Kathy Casey's Northwest Table

OREGON · WASHINGTON · BRITISH COLUMBIA · SOUTHERN ALASKA

BY KATHY CASEY

∘ ∘ ∘

Food Photographs by E. Jane Armstrong

Scenic Photographs by Mike Hipple and Joel W. Rogers

CHRONICLE BOOKS
SAN FRANCISCO

E. JANE ARMSTRONG: Pages 2, 34 (entire top and middle rows, bottom row right and left), 37, 41, 48, 57, 67, 70, 72 (upper left, upper center, middle row left, bottom row right), 76, 81, 87, 92, 97, 98 (top left, middle row center), 103, 106, 113, 119, 126, 132 (top right and bottom center), 135, 136, 140, 146, 151, 156, 162, 166 (top right, middle row left, bottom row center, bottom row right), 171, 174, 177, 183, 187, 192 (top left and center, middle row left and right), 201, 204, 210, 212, and 216.

MIKE HIPPLE: Pages 5, 6, 8, 10, 13, 14, 17, 19, 20, 21, 23, 24, 25, 31, 34 (bottom row center), 39, 53, 72 (upper right, middle row center and right, bottom row left and center), 85, 90, 98 (top row center and right, middle row left and right, bottom row left and center), 132 (top left and center, entire middle row, bottom row left and right), 166 (top row left and center, middle row center and right, bottom row left), 181, 189, 192 (top right, middle row center, entire bottom row), 197, 199, 207, 215, 226, and 232.

JOEL W. ROGERS: Pages 26, 27, 54, 61, 98 (bottom right), and 125.

Library of Congress Cataloging-in-Publication Data available.

ISBN-10: 0-8118-5432-9
ISBN-13: 978-0-8118-5432-0

Manufactured in China.

Editor: Ann E. Manly
Design: Gretchen Scoble
Food Styling: Diana Isaiou, Patty Wittmann, Charlotte Omnès, Jean Galton

Distributed in Canada by Raincoast Books
9050 Shaughnessy Street
Vancouver, British Columbia V6P 6E5

10 9 8 7 6 5 4 3 2 1

Chronicle Books LLC
85 Second Street
San Francisco, California 94105

www.chroniclebooks.com

Kathy Casey's Northwest Table

I would like to dedicate this book to the memory of my mom,
Eunice Pavletich Baker, and grandmother, "Mimi" Katherine Washburn,
who put an apron on me as soon as I could stand and taught me to
cook with the bounty of our great Northwest.

At Seattle's Pike Place Market on a rainy day

CONTENTS

ACKNOWLEDGMENTS

A meal is not made great by just one dish or ingredient, nor is a cookbook created by one person. It took a "kitchen full" of associates' talents and tribulations to help me get this book done.

I would like to thank foremost Ann Manly, a longtime associate and friend, for her diligent editing and for the extreme talent she brings to this book. From long nights of revising to long days of research and testing—all with tight deadlines—she is always there. Thank you, Ann; you are five-star.

More thanks goes to chef Mindy Hankins of Kathy Casey Food Studios, for her whirlwind of recipe-testing and her great palate and support; to sous-chef Lindsey Malland, for her testing assistance and taste buds; to Studios business manager Amanda Coate, for her help with research and for organizing and coordinating "everyone"; to senior beverage associate and master mixologist Ryan Magarian, for his cocktail collaboration; to chef Janice Vaughns of Dish D'Lish, for making sure everything is always tip-top; and to former associate Jason Gregory, for his knowledge of Northwest microbrews and for taste-testing. Also much thanks goes to Chronicle Books editorial director Bill LeBlond, for asking me to do this book and for his creative insights; to associate editor Amy Treadwell for her guidance and support; and to the rest of the Chronicle team for their enthusiasm and dedication to this book.

For bringing to life the beauty of food on these pages, I thank the ever-so-talented food photographer E. Jane Armstrong, and Armstrong Photography studio director Scott Pitts, along with the team of food stylists: Diana Isaiou, Patty Wittmann, Charlotte Omnès, and Jean Galton. The fantastic and artful scenic photography was made possible by the talent of Mike Hipple, who was always willing to head out with his camera to shoot the summer's bounty as quickly as it came into fruit. And many thanks go to Joel W. Rogers for his beautiful supporting scenic photography.

I would like to thank my loving husband, John Casey, who served, as always, as chief taste-tester and personal supporter.

Last but not least, thank you, Gretchen Scoble, for your fantastic design work that brings the talents of everyone else together so very beautifully.

< Developing clouds over Puget Sound along Washington's Chuckanut Drive

LIVING IN THE BEAUTIFUL NORTHWEST

Growing up in Seattle and living in the Northwest for most of my life, I couldn't imagine living anywhere else. Other parts of the country are wonderful, too—don't get me wrong—but there is something that gets in your blood here. Some say it's moss! But maybe it's the four distinct seasons we are blessed with.

The sunny summers—when it stays light out till 10 P.M. or in Alaska 24/7!—are just hot enough. And as the days begin to shorten, the summers often turn into crisp Indian summers where the sun shines brightly during the day but the air is brisk and cool. As the year slides slowly into fall, the trees turn brilliant colors, then drop their leaves, making crisp piles to jump into. Then the rain starts, and the skies turn gray, and Northwesterners turn to their espresso for cold-weather pick-me-ups. The first fresh snow falls on the mountain crests, and the early nightfall signals winter. When we turn the corner into spring, gentle showers are upon us—yes, more rain—but the sun starts to peek out and the trees and flowers start to bloom, waking us up from our winter blues.

At every turn of the calendar's pages, we look forward to what the next season brings to our kitchens, from spring's asparagus, morels, and lamb to summer's berries, salmon, peaches, and tomatoes to fall's apples, chanterelles, hazelnuts, pumpkins, and squash, and finally to winter's oysters. We celebrate the riches of the beautiful Northwest on our tables year-round.

Is There a Northwest Cuisine? Well, of Course There Is! Northwest cuisine embodies the bounty of the region and the spirit and life-style of the people. While there may not be one definitive dish, Northwest cuisine surely is about fresh seasonal ingredients and the creative yet informal attitudes of its cooks, chefs, and food enthusiasts.

What Is a Typical Northwestern Meal? It could be like one I had last summer. My neighbor had just gotten back from crabbing and brought over three live, meaty Dungeness crabs. I did the neighborly trade thing, reciprocating with jars of freshly preserved marionberry jam. That night's dinner began with tasty Quillisascut chèvre, along with my Blueberry Lavender Chutney, spread on Essential Baking Company crackers for a premeal nibble, moved on to fresh Crab Louis salads with homemade dressing accompanied by big glasses of crisp Chinook sauvignon blanc, and then finished with little bowls of fresh raspberries and juicy apricots. Yum!

Or perhaps it is a meal I had last spring. A Copper River salmon, caught just twenty-four hours previously by a "friend's friend" who owns a small two-person commercial fishing vessel in Cordova, Alaska, was flown to Seattle and brought to my Studios. I panseared the fish and served it with sautéed morel mushrooms and unembellished steamed asparagus from Eastern Washington. Honey-baked rhubarb mousse was that night's dessert.

Then again, it might be the Sunday roast lamb my mom made with baked apples; or a fondly remembered weekend breakfast of Swedish pancakes with lingonberries; or a lingcod a chef colleague braised in coconut milk and Thai herbs.

On the other hand, it might be a quickie take-out lunch from the teriyaki shop around the corner; crisp tostadas topped with seviche and fresh salsa spiked with chiles and cilantro; a big sub layered with locally cured meats; or a weekday morning's faststart cranberry muffin and double-tall latte.

‹ Snow-capped North Cascades above the Stehekin River

Is This Northwest Cuisine? As a born-and-raised-here gal, I say it's all Northwest cuisine. But if I had to summarize and put it into words, I'd say the cuisine is fresh, bright-flavored cooking that draws on the bounty of the seasons, simply prepared, with some Asian influences peppered here and there. Throughout the region, our cooking reflects these characteristic features: the centrality of salmon to our cultural history and spirit; the generous use of the berries that grow in the mountains and the mushrooms that pop up in our moss-fuzzy forest floors; the support for farmers and ranchers who grow our peaches, hazelnuts, and other beautiful produce; and the respect for the clean waters of the rivers and bays, streams and estuaries where fish and shellfish abound.

Appreciation of the outdoors is widespread here; and when the sun does shine, we all head outside, firing up our grills and dining alfresco anytime we can. When friends get together, everyone brings a dish they can flaunt, to be eaten with a main course of thick juicy steaks, pork or lamb chops, or vibrant-colored salmon fillets. Cherry mojitos, local beers, Northwest wines, and conversation flow as even a little bit of sun puts extra smiles on our faces.

People here still "put things up." From as far back as I can remember, my family was always going picking for something. My mom loved to tell the story that, when I was five, I picked a whole flat of strawberries. From early spring through late fall, Northwest cooks are freezing and smoking salmon, jamming berries, canning peaches, making vinegar out of blueberries, or drying venison jerky. By preserving the seasonal cornucopia, we can savor our beloved foods year-round.

And who wouldn't take pleasure in a bowl of honey-sweetened yogurt topped with crisp granola and preserved wild huckleberries on a chilly winter morning?

Many different ethnic traditions are woven into Northwest cuisine. Consider, for example, preparations of the region's emblematic fish, salmon: wood-planking over an open fire comes from a Native American method; gravlax is typical of the Scandinavian immigrants; and teriyaki was introduced by the Japanese. Lamb dishes show similarly diverse origins, from the English and Scots colonists' shepherd's pie to Basque pimiento-laced stews to the curries brought by East Indian immigrants. Located on the Pacific Rim, the region has been prominent in the development of Asian-fusion food. And for the past three decades or so, Pacific Northwest cuisine has been "feeling the heat." The influx of Southeast Asian foods has reinforced the already-present Mexican influences; now, marinades for salmon and sauces for oysters regularly contain chipotle chiles or sambal oelek.

The Northwest palate is ever-changing, with new preferences arising as different peoples move into the region and old standbys are being passed along to keep our delicious traditions alive to be appreciated by generations to come.

THE REGION

The Pacific Northwest is not only budding with culinary ingenuity but also with vision and originality in other fields. British Columbia has a booming film industry known as "Hollywood of the North," and IBM's largest innovations center is there. Oregon has Nike as well as Columbia Sportswear, one of the world's largest outerwear brands. Washington is home to online-shopping-giant Amazon and to Boeing Commercial Airplanes, Microsoft, and Starbucks. All this inspiration must come from somewhere . . . maybe it's the good food here that gets the creative juices flowing.

But all work and no play? Hardly! In a place with this much imagination, there has to be some fantastic fun, too! Opportunities for activity are everywhere, both indoors and out. We have a thriving music scene as well as vigorous theater and arts organizations and highly regarded museums and galleries. And outdoor adventure is only about forty-five minutes from any Northwest city. We have innumerable trails for hiking and biking; lakes, streams, and rivers for fishing; wondrous mountains for skiing and climbing; sites rich with marine life for diving explorations; and beautiful, expansive waters for boating and kayaking. It is nearly impossible to get bored living in the Northwest!

I certainly have been on my share of Northwest escapades . . . usually in pursuit of delicious rewards. I've hiked through Alaskan wild tundra in hip boots—trying to keep up with my six-foot-tall companions—while on the way to fish for the illustrious salmon. I've tromped through the deep, lush forests of Oregon in search of chanterelles; on one such outing, my fellow pickers and I hit pay dirt with more than ninety pounds of the golden treasure. In British Columbia's Campbell River, I donned a wet suit and bodysurfed through the whitecaps to swim side by side with the salmon—definitely an experience never to be forgotten.

And, as Washington is my backyard, I have had plenty of adventures right here—gathering wild huckleberries in the Cascade foothills, fishing for salmon in Puget Sound, roasting oysters on the beach, picking enormous morel mushrooms in burned-out forests, fishing glacier lakes for cutthroat trout so plentiful they almost jumped up out of the water at you, and harvesting bushels of tree fruit east of the mountains.

Experiences such as these, along with friends, farmers, fishers, and producers, have inspired the recipes in this book.

Lookout at Lummi Island, Washington

Seattle coffee drinker and Space Needle

THE URBAN CENTERS: PORTLAND, SEATTLE, AND VANCOUVER

The Northwest is food-centric. Restaurants flourish in Vancouver, Seattle, and Portland as well as in smaller cities. From mom-and-pop cafes serving up big hearty breakfasts of thick-cut smoked bacon, farm-fresh eggs, and whole-grain toast with mouth-watering berry jams, to chef-entrepreneurs' fine-dining establishments featuring inspired Northwest cuisine and sustainable food products to a wealth of ethnic restaurants offering exotic soon-to-be-the-rage dishes, there is always somewhere new to tempt urban foodies in search of something delicious.

The least populous of the Northwest's metropolitan areas, Portland nevertheless has its share of cutting-edge, innovative restaurants and bars started by passionate entrepreneurs. Even the "big boys" get into the act; you'll find homegrown fast-food chains serving local products: Oregon natural beef burgers topped with Tillamook Cheddar, and toasted-hazelnut milk shakes. In Portland's smaller, single-property restaurants, chefs are almost fanatical about knowing where their ingredients come from and who grows or raises them. These ardent chefs have a one-on-one relationship with their culinary producing partners. The chefs list their sources on their menus and in the titles of their dishes and are constantly on the lookout for the new and unusual from tiny farmsteads and boutique producers. This part of the region has always been known as a bit more "crunchy" than its counterparts, but the attitude serves the city and its restaurant patrons well, as we look toward eating healthier and more locally.

Seattle is known nationally for its impassioned chefs and unique restaurants. The city and its suburbs lay claim to just about every kind of Asian restaurant, and the Pacific Rim influence is clearly seen—from the incorporation of no-longer-mysterious ingredients to ingenious reinterpretations of classic dishes. In the past few years, Seattle's neighborhoods have become as likely sites as downtown for destination dining. Newly hip Ballard, historic Columbia City, and funky Fremont are just a few of the 'hoods that now pull in fans from all over the metropolis. Seattle also offers a range of late-night dining, attracting club-closing indie-band scenesters and after-show theater-, opera-, and symphony-goers alike. Food-lovers are always in pursuit of the hottest "find"—where is the most authentic Latin food; where is that new bistro opening? Seattle also goes for a social style of participatory eating: little plates to share while sipping cocktails, bites of *doro wat* to pinch up with center-of-the-table sourdough *injera*, or Vietnamese summer rolls to assemble at the table with rice paper sheets dipped in warm water. And even though locals have grown up eating salmon, they still adore this fish. At waterside eateries, tables are filled with the hungry after-work crowd, often seated side by side with local fishermen; grilled salmon is served along with iced plates of just-shucked briny oysters and pints of microbrews.

Vancouver is the heartbeat of British Columbia, Canada's third largest province. Chic and sophisticated, Vancouver embodies a rich tapestry of ethnic cultures. Tourists and food-lovers alike flock to the Granville Island Market, and eager shoppers head to Robson Street to check out what's new and hip. For the best dim sum in the West, proceed east to Chinatown, where live king crabs are displayed in saltwater tanks. South of downtown is Little India, where shops selling fragrant spices and colorful silks line the streets. Gastown, the city's oldest district, is known for its colorful nightlife scene. Tourists and passengers from nearby cruise-ship facilities, drawn to the area's restaurants and shops in renovated warehouses, have energized its rediscovery. You can find a different cuisine at nearly every turn of the street in the Northwest's most cosmopolitan city.

If you don't live in the Northwest but are planning to visit, then I urge you to explore the vibrant culinary scene with a sense of boldness. Don't do the touristy things. Pick up a local weekly newspaper from a sidewalk box to see what the residents are doing and where they're headed for the weekend, or check out an online chat room for the area. Visit a restaurant you would never try ordinarily and order something new. Be adventurous! If you are from the area, visit a new neighborhood. Challenge yourself to get out of your culinary comfort zone. You may find your new must-have food or have your most exciting gustatory encounter ever—you will never know until you try!

WEST OF THE CASCADES: THE VALLEYS

The fabled waters of the Pacific Northwest are among the region's defining attributes, and the agriculture of each state and province is made possible by major rivers that drain the glaciers and mountain springs. West of the Cascades, this runoff is carried by the Fraser River in British Columbia, the Skagit in Washington, and the Willamette in Oregon, to name only a few. A fruitful valley lies beside each.

The nineteenth-century pioneers who came across the more than two thousand miles of the Oregon Trail were lured by the "promised land" that lay at the end of that arduous journey, the Willamette Valley. The narrow valley is bordered by temperate rain forest and blessed with a mild climate; its 120-mile-long namesake river runs through fertile land. There are more covered bridges in the valley than anywhere else west of the Mississippi, but this valley is really known for its diverse agriculture: from nuts, pears, flowers, and Christmas trees to pinot noir and pinot gris wine grapes to an abundance of berry farms. The region acknowledges its plenitude with a multitude of festivals, celebrating irises, filberts, hops, and beer.

Washington's Skagit Valley, too, is a historical mecca for farmers. At the beginning of the twentieth century, there were as many as nine hundred dairies; today there are fewer than fifty. However, more and more small organic farms are popping up, in connection with the sustainable and natural foods movement. Organic farmers in this fertile valley, known as Magic Skagit, raise beef, make cheese, and grow berries, herbs, pumpkins, and apples. While in years past, peas were a major crop, today it's red potatoes. Larger producers grow much of the supply of vegetable seed—about half the world's beet and Brussels sprout seeds, along with parsley, cabbage, parsnip, Chinese cabbage, and mustard seeds. The Skagit is also the world's largest bulb producer and is known for its riot of color in the spring when the fields are awash with vivid tulips, and "Sunday drivers" flock to take pictures and admire the beauty of this luxuriant valley.

In British Columbia's picturesque, productive, and verdant Fraser Valley, there is also a movement to teach consumers about where their food is farmed and by whom. The Fraser Valley Farm Direct Marketing Association strives to build a relationship between farms and their customers. The valley lies between the Coast Mountains and the Cascades, and more than half of British Columbia's agricultural production is generated there from its crops of berries, fruit, eggs, poultry, vegetables, nursery stock, turf mushrooms, and dairy products. On another side of the growing realm is British Columbia's hothouse industry—growers of hydroponic tomatoes, cucumbers, and peppers that reach tables across the Northwest and beyond.

In addition to their usefulness in agriculture, the rivers that run through these valleys have supported major salmon runs and were prime fishing waters in years past. In the Fraser River still to this day lurks the prehistoric-looking white sturgeon; however, it is now endangered and the sport fishery is strictly catch and release. With more emerging awareness of sustainability of these precious resources, the five salmon species, steelhead, and trout can be fished as stocks permit.

Historically counterposed, agricultural interests and salmon recovery efforts may now begin to converge. The onslaught of asphalt and concrete threatens both salmon habitat and rural land. Ironically, it may turn out that modified agricultural practices could help to save the salmon in the long run.

Still, with urban sprawl and population increasing, it is a fight to keep the farmlands of these beautiful regions from turning into another housing development. It will undoubtedly continue to be a struggle, even though many concerned groups and farm organizations are taking on the cause to save our farmlands west of the mountains. It's a battle worth waging.

Along Oregon's famous "Fruit Loop" drive through the Hood River Valley ›

COASTAL BEACHES

From Oregon to British Columbia and southern Alaska, the coastline offers breathtaking scenery, with the winds, tide, sun, and rain making for a different seascape every day. Some beaches are long and sandy, with occasional giant dunes. Others are jagged and rocky with rugged cliffs. Sea stack rocks rise dramatically out of the sea. Some beaches require a challenging hike to reach, while others are right there for the strolling.

There are activities to please all, depending on the season or the beach. Except for the most resilient outdoors person, the waters are usually too icy cold for swimming, so many keep their activities to lying out in the sun, birding, exploring tide pools, or whale watching. Amusements that are more vigorous include kite flying, clamming, tossing Frisbees, and seaweed fights with big sea kelp "carrots." Some beaches are known for surfing and others for glass-float collecting. Winter storm-watchers witness the ocean whipped into a frenzy, see huge waves crash spectacularly against the rocks, and gape as gigantic driftwood logs smash onto the beach.

Washington's most popular coastal spots are Ocean Shores, the Long Beach Peninsula, and Westport. On up the Olympic Peninsula are Port Angeles and Dungeness Spit, which sticks out five miles into the Strait of Juan de Fuca. On many childhood visits to Ocean Shores, I wondered why we were vacationing at the beach with our coats on over our bathing suits and shorts! Summer on the coast of the Pacific Northwest might not be the warmest trip you can take, but I happily remember lazy days of combing the beach for shells and the beautiful, fragile sand dollars. Looking back, I am sure it was the relaxing lapping of the waves that brought the adults back every summer.

We also went south on our summer beach ventures, and my happiest trips were to the Oregon town of Seaside, where there were many more exciting activities for the younger crew. I remember horseback riding along the shore, with the wind whipping in my hair and the crisp salt air filling my lungs. And I still recall a dinner where we had Oregon bay shrimp cocktails followed by big juicy fried scallops served with tangy sweet coleslaw, lemony tartar sauce, and thick slices of fresh-baked bread. Afterward, we ate saltwater taffy in flavors like huckleberry and molasses.

My most recent beach trip was to Tofino, a very small town on the west coast of Vancouver Island. Though summer is the busiest season there, my trip was in the winter and we watched a most spectacular storm. Well bundled up, we walked the shore while nibbling on famed Nanaimo bars and sipping cups of steaming coffee. The area is just as intriguing in springtime during the Pacific Rim Whale Festival. Tofino and its sister town, Ucluelet, hold the celebration from mid-March to mid-April to commemorate the annual migration of almost twenty thousand Pacific gray whales, which pass along the coast of Vancouver Island as they make their way from Mexico to Alaska.

On the southwest corner of British Columbia's mainland is the Sunshine Coast, a 110-mile stretch that winds from the Strait of Georgia all the way to Desolation Sound. Much different from the gray skies that characterize much of the coastal Northwest, the Sunshine Coast averages two thousand hours of annual sunshine. Its old-growth forest, alpine peaks, marine parks, and marshland bird sanctuaries attract a community of unhurried folks and inspire an extraordinary society of artists, musicians, potters, glass blowers, and writers.

Rocky shores en route to Vancouver, British Columbia ›

THE ISLANDS

Thousands of islands dot the Pacific coast from Oregon to Alaska. Many of them are tiny and uninhabited; some, designated as wilderness areas, are closed to human beings to protect the wildlife and fragile plants. The larger islands, however, are peopled by both year-round residents and seasonal visitors.

Ferries connect the vast array of islands and form the standard transportation grid for both work and play. A trip to the Northwest would not be complete without a ferry ride. Whether on a quick jaunt across Puget Sound or a long, luxurious ride through the Queen Charlottes or San Juans, passengers take in the vistas—from icy mountain views to quaint villages to the occasional barking sea lion or pod of orca whales.

The magnificent Inside Passage follows the island-protected waterways from Seattle to Skagway, Alaska; this is the route that was taken by gold-seekers in the 1800s. Today, cruise ships touting gourmet menus and fine wines to eager sightseers equipped with binoculars and cameras weave through the Passage on journeys to the blue glaciers of Alaska.

Smaller vessels also ply these waters. Kayakers pack hearty lunches of locally made bread and cheese to fuel their day trips between islands. Recreational mariners hopeful of catching a seafood feast load fishing tackle, crab pots, and clam guns for summer sailing excursions. Many a boat-side supper consists of fresh-cracked crab, hot garlic bread, a crisp green salad, and cold microbrews or clanking glasses of sauvignon blanc.

While the Queen Charlotte Islands, a sportfishing heaven, are one of the most remote areas of British Columbia, Vancouver Island has a population of about 750,000. Victoria, the provincial capital and western Canada's oldest city, is located here. This charming city, named in honor of Queen Victoria, celebrates its British heritage with aplomb. Called the "City of Gardens," Victoria is world renowned for its beautiful Victorian-inspired gardens that are green year-round in the gentle climate. Taking tea is another British custom in the city, and afternoon tea service is an unforgettable feature of the stately Empress Hotel. What fun to nibble cucumber-and-smoked-salmon finger sandwiches and tiny scones dolloped with Devonshire cream while sipping tea from fine bone china!

Blue skies reflect upon water

Typical Northwest island transportation

The numerous Gulf Islands lie in the Strait of Georgia between Vancouver Island and mainland British Columbia; this serene, tranquil environment is an artists' haven where organic produce is grown, candles are hand-dipped, and sweaters are knitted from naturally dyed artisan-spun wool. To the south, the archipelago continues as the San Juan Islands in Puget Sound, separated only by the international boundary. A comparable moderate climate and similarly easygoing existence typify life in the San Juans.

The islands are home to some of our region's most inspired restaurants. Menus are created around what comes to the back door that morning: matsutake pine mushrooms, small Manila clams, and garlic chives, for example, turn into an appetizer of steamed clams with shaved matsutakes. Or herb-crusted island lamb rack with a ragout of chanterelles. The islands are a chef's paradise.

FORESTS AND MOUNTAINS

The mountain ranges of the Northwest vary in environment from dusty high desert to moss-draped rain forest. And each of the variations presents recreational possibilities. Our mountains and accessible foothills, from the rugged peaks of the North Cascades to the cascading waterfalls along the Columbia River gorge to the crest of Mount Hood, entice skiers and snowboarders, fishers, climbers and hikers, rockhounds, and hot-spring "soakers."

The Cascades are the best known of the Northwest's mountain ranges. These snowcapped mountains start in northern California and continue up into British Columbia. The highest is Mount Rainier, a challenging climb for even the most conditioned climber. But probably the most notorious is Mount St. Helens, an active volcano that woke up again in 1980. Many of the Cascade volcanoes, previously considered dormant, are now thought to be just "resting." The Northwest's premier skiing destination is Whistler in British Columbia, known for its "powder" and its après-ski party scene where many an appetizing Northwest spread is set out.

The Alaska Range is another esteemed recreational setting. Mount McKinley, the tallest mountain in North America, is located there in Denali National Park. On my biggest Alaskan adventure, my group drove to McKinley, then—while the guys in the party hiked—I flew in to our fishing destination and was awestruck at the majestic beauty of this Northwest landmark.

The varied terrain and habitats in the region's mountains and foothills also afford some excellent hunting, especially the high desert country. Elk and deer roasts, homemade venison sausages, pheasants, quail, duck, and even wild turkey are found in the Northwest hunter's freezer. Canadians celebrate the holidays with Canadian goose or duck stuffed with apples and huckleberries.

Day trips and camping trips to the mountains commonly lead to some tasty foraging. Being an avid forager myself, I love it that you can jump in the car and be in the forest in less than an hour. My pals and I always pack a portable burner and a big frying pan along with some olive oil, kosher salt, and a few herbs. We also throw in some good bread, cheese, fruit chutney, and wine, of course.

A friend from Oregon tells me not only of fishing trips for steelhead, German brown trout, and freshwater sturgeon but also of boyhood crawfish-trapping and frog-hunting with homemade spears and flashlights! The excursion's catch was fried up in butter by Mom the next evening.

He also recollects finding the delicate-tasting shaggy mane mushroom—so determined to surface that it can push up through the pavement of mountain roads. In the late summer, purple huckleberries dot the hillsides. It's hard not to eat as many as you pick, but you know you've had a good day when your baskets are full and your fingers purple. And if the terrain is just right, there will also be ripe wild blueberries. Later in the fall comes a mycophagist's (mushroom-eater's) fantasy when mushrooms poke their elusive heads out of the forest floor.

My favorite foraging meal after a strenuous day of hiking and picking in the woods—if we were lucky—is a big batch of sautéed mushrooms eaten right from the pan, scooped up on slices of rustic bread and washed down with a well-deserved glass of wine. Whether you've garnered fish, berries, or mushrooms from our bountiful mountains, you can enjoy your reward right there in the fresh forest air. Nothing's ever tasted better.

A forest's peek at Oregon's Mt. Hood ›

OVER THE MOUNTAINS TO THE DESERT

People from west of the Cascades who have never driven "over the mountains" can't believe the change in the landscape when they do. Just after you cross through our mountain passes, poof! The lush greenery is gone, replaced by desert. The farther you venture east, the more frequently tumbleweeds will dance across the highway and sagebrush dapple the countryside.

Eastern Washington is the breadbasket of the state, boasting some of the most fertile ground in the nation; wheat is one of the state's major crops. This desert area, including southeastern British Columbia and northeastern Oregon, is agriculturally productive because of water diverted from the mighty Columbia and its vast expanse of tributaries. In the United States, a network of hydroelectric dams generates most of the Northwest's power and regulates the water quenching the thirst of some of the country's richest farmland.

The rich volcanic soil is planted with crops such as apples, potatoes, peas, hops, cherries, lentils, peaches, and apricots. In addition, small farms, increasingly organic, specialize in heirloom tomatoes, eggplants, peanuts, and peppers. Rows of hops that reach up to the skies grow over an inch an hour in hot, hot summer temperatures that sometimes reach 120 degrees!

But not all agriculture in the high desert is farm crops. With chefs and consumers turning toward natural and organic meats,

there are more and more small operations as well as larger cooperatives raising beef, pork, and lamb. Country Natural Beef is a great example of a cooperative of about seventy family ranchers committed to growing cattle free of growth hormones and feed antibiotics. It is notable as the only natural beef program in the United States where individual ranchers are directly responsible to the meat manager and the end customer for both the eating quality of the product and claims on growing practices.

The eastern side of the Northwest is where I have had some of my most memorable meals. The best hamburger I've ever had would have to be a "Squiggy burger." The beef was from a grass-fed steer raised by friends on a small farm in Prosser, Washington, and given apples and corncobs as treats. Also etched in my taste memory is a feast at our wine-maker companions' vineyard. It started with chilled sparkling wine from their experimental personal stash; along with it, we luxuriated in some Columbia River sturgeon caviar on crostini. The meal continued with grilled salmon that I had caught the day before off Whidbey Island with my dad. The salmon was topped with a Bing cherry salsa made with just-picked cherries and accompanied with baby yellow and green squash and tiny steamed potatoes just dug from the garden. It was a meal like no other—enjoyed with our friends' luscious merlot. Knowing where your food comes from is important, and the care and dedication to quality come through in the taste.

Never-ending fields of wheat

ALASKA: THE LAST FRONTIER

The largest state of the union, Alaska is thought of as the last frontier and the place where pioneer spirit still abounds.

Near the end of the nineteenth century, gold was discovered in Alaska, and more than sixty thousand eager Americans traveled north to make their big fortune. But circumstances in the Klondike were hard, the trails were too steep for pack animals, and the gold lay under permafrost. Many lost their lives; few struck it rich.

Steller sea lions rest on glacial ice floes in Alaska's Inside Passage

However, the gold rush did contribute to Alaskan cuisine. Facing extreme conditions, eager prospectors did not have much fresh food, and their travels took them far from civilization for long periods. Being survivors, the prospectors learned how to make and use sour- dough. This naturally fermented yeast starter could be kept alive by a daily "feeding" with flour. These sourdough starters were a man's lifeblood and so were kept close at his side to keep them "alive." Stories have it that on bone-chilling nights prospectors tucked their starters inside their shirts to keep the culture warm. Sourdough starters were used for making the best pancakes or flapjacks ever—especially when spread with wild blueberry jam. Today, Alaskan sourdough is still a tasty tradition.

And ever since the gold rush days, Alaska has symbolized wide-open economic opportunity. High-school classmates left their safe and cozy Washington and Oregon homes after graduation to head out to the stormy and treacherous Alaskan seas to crab, hoping to make their fortunes. Just about every local young man has spent a season or a summer in the rough waters of Alaska. Guys returning home lugged boxes and boxes of king crabmeat—so plentiful in those days that much of it ended up in macaroni salad at picnics! Young women I know worked in the canneries in summertime; they lived in tents and cleaned salmon for twenty hours a day. Some of them to this day will still not eat salmon.

Today, Alaska is most known for its seafood and its great outdoor adventures. Visitors, fishers, hikers, and nature-lovers lured to this still untamed state are awed by the pristine waters, glaciers, snowcapped mountains, and deep forests where there are amazing chances to view an assortment of flora and fauna. In the rugged outlying terrain, wildlife by far outnumbers people. And, while the cities might be somewhat heavily populated, the wide-ranging wildlife is there, too. A well-known Anchorage restaura- teur and super-outdoorsman told me that, when he was jogging in his neighborhood one day, he was chased for blocks by a massive Alaskan moose!

Bears are numerous here and love to dine on salmon. You'll reliably see bald eagles diving for their favorite meal of salmon as well. These rich fish have a superior fat content that gives them their buttery opulence and high nutrient level. Alaska salmon are known throughout the world as very fine fish. No wonder so many creatures want to eat them!

In many other places where salmon were once abundant, stocks have deteriorated, but in Alaska, this revered fish is still plentiful. The state constitution actually requires that salmon habitat be protected. The Marine Stewardship Council, an inde- pendent global nonprofit organization that promotes responsible fishing practices, announced in 2000 that Alaska salmon is the first United States fishery to be certified as sustainable.

In the big cities, you can always tell when a flight has come in from Alaska. Oversize fish boxes careen down the ramp to the luggage carousel, and unshaven passengers in Carhartts pace, antsy to collect their catches and take their prizes home for a Northwest salmon dinner.

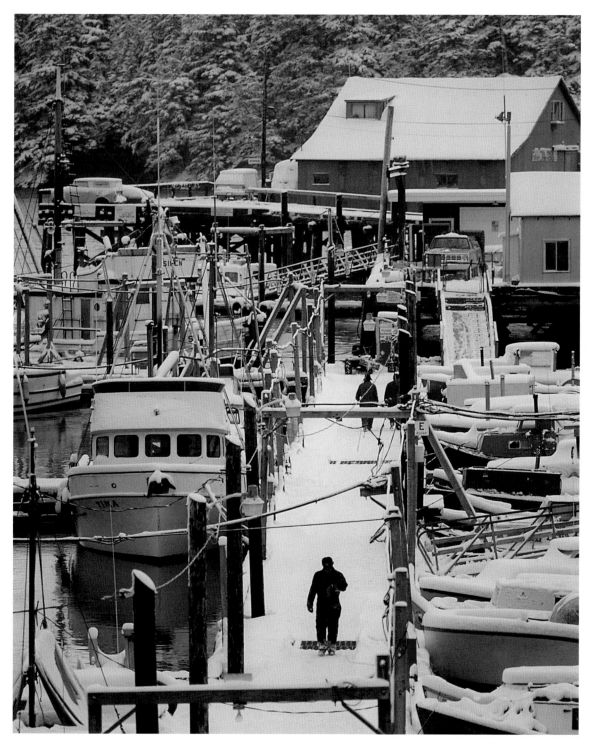

Winter snowfall, Cordova, Alaska

GENERAL RECIPE NOTES

When trying a recipe for the first time, be sure to read through the whole recipe. Next, get all your ingredients out and ready to start. I like to cut and measure everything ahead of time, basically making a "kit," then double-check my work one last time and proceed onward from there.

Cooking is an art, not a science; ovens and burner strengths vary, as do ingredients from different parts of the country. Use your best judgment when making the recipes in this book.

ASSUMPTIONS

Bell peppers are seeded and deribbed.

Chiles are seeded and deribbed but, if you like more heat, leave in the seeds and ribs.

Crabmeat. Generally, there is no need to pick through purchased fresh Dungeness crabmeat for shell particles; if you are substituting lump crab or another crabmeat, be sure to do so.

Foil is aluminum foil.

The whole green onion is used unless the recipe specifies "white part only" or "tops."

When herbs are minced or in whole-leaf form, they are specified as fresh or dried, but when used in bunches or as sprigs, they are assumed to be fresh. To substitute dried herbs for fresh, use only 1/3 to 1/2 as much; but substitute only if you're in a pinch, as this will greatly affect a recipe's flavor.

Medium size is assumed for fruits and vegetables unless otherwise specified.

Paprika is available in a range of pungency from sweet to hot, and smoked Spanish paprika (pimentón) is available sweet, bittersweet, or hot; if not specified in the recipe, use what you like.

Parmesan cheese. Buy blocks of the best you can find and afford; Parmigiano-Reggiano is certainly the first choice. You can shave block Parmesan with a regular vegetable peeler if you don't have a fancy cheese knife.

Prawns vs. shrimp terminology. On the West Coast, we tend to refer to all larger-size shrimp as prawns and to the tiny cooked salad, or bay, shrimp as shrimp. One recipe calls for "spot prawns"; these are large prawns available seasonally in the Northwest; any large shrimp, 16 to 20 or fewer per pound, will do.

Salad greens. When you rinse salad greens, be sure to dry them well using a salad spinner.

"Season to taste" means for you to taste the dish and then adjust the seasoning by adding more salt if you so desire and pepper if the recipe indicates pepper.

"Store refrigerated" means to cover or wrap before refrigerating, unless otherwise noted. (Be sure food is cooled before covering.)

UNLESS SPECIFIED OTHERWISE IN INDIVIDUAL RECIPES:

Brown sugar is always measured "packed."

Butter is salted.

Cream is heavy whipping cream.

Eggs are large.

Flour is all-purpose.

Fresh ginger is peeled.

Garlic is always fresh—not the kind in a jar!

Leeks—only the white part is used.

Milk is whole milk. Generally, you can substitute 2% but not fat-free—the lack of butterfat might have an adverse effect on the results of the recipe.

Onions are yellow unless specified white or red.

Onions, potatoes, garlic, and carrots are peeled.

Parsley can be either flat-leaf or curly; use what you like.

Salt is your choice. Most chefs prefer kosher and/or sea salt and often use these rather than table salt. You'd be surprised at the difference in flavor and texture from one salt to the next; use what you have on hand, but you might want to consider adding kosher or sea salt to your cupboard if it's not already there.

Soy sauce is regular-strength Japanese-style soy sauce, such as Kikkoman.

Sugar is granulated.

CUTS

Chop: To cut into $\frac{1}{4}$-inch to $\frac{1}{2}$-inch irregular pieces that have a rustic look; pieces are not precisely cubed.

Coarsely chop: $\frac{1}{2}$-inch rough-cut pieces, except when referring to fresh herbs, such as flat-leaf parsley, and small foods, such as nuts or olives; in those cases, "coarsely chop" means rough-cutting into about $\frac{1}{4}$-inch pieces.

Finely chop: $\frac{1}{8}$-inch to $\frac{1}{4}$-inch pieces.

Dice: To cut foods into small cubes; the very even cuts make for even cooking and an appealing look; the size is usually specified, for example, $\frac{1}{4}$ inch or $\frac{1}{2}$ inch.

Julienne: To cut into even, matchstick-size strips, 2 to 3 inches long and $\frac{1}{16}$-inch-square in cross-section, or the specified size.

Mince: To cut into very small pieces, about $\frac{1}{8}$ inch or smaller.

Very finely mince: $\frac{1}{16}$ inch or smaller.

TIPS & PRACTICALITIES

To make crème fraîche: If you cannot locate this culture-thickened cream in your area, you can make your own. Put 1 cup sour cream and 2 cups heavy cream in a large glass jar. Tighten the lid and shake to combine thoroughly. Set in a warm place for 8 to 24 hours until thickened.

To make lemon or other citrus zest: Zest is the outer peel of the fruit—with no white pith attached. You can remove the zest from the fruit with a fine zesting tool that makes long, very thin, pretty strands, or you can peel off the zest with an ordinary potato peeler, being sure not to get any white pith, and then finely cut the zest in very, very thin long strips or mince it. Or you can grate it off. For this method, I like to use a Microplane. Be careful; this tool is very, very sharp. Don't grate deep enough to get into the white pith.

To debeard mussels: Grab and pull off the fuzzy part that attaches them to rocks. Then scrub the shells clean and rinse in clear water. If you have trouble getting the beards off, whip out your pliers—they work wonders!

To roast peppers: Roast bell peppers or chiles under a gas-flame broiler, on a grill rack over hot coals, or in a preheated 475°F oven. Turn the peppers as necessary until the skin is charred black on all sides. Immediately place in a plastic bag or covered bowl for 15 minutes. When cool enough to handle, slip the skins off the peppers and remove the seeds. When peeling and seeding chiles, wear rubber gloves. Substitute with canned or jarred roasted peppers.

To toast nuts: Spread them on a baking sheet and toast in a preheated 350°F oven for about 6 to 8 minutes, or until golden.

For hazelnuts, you will probably want to rub off the skin. When the toasted nuts are cool enough to handle, put the hazelnuts in a clean non-fuzzy dish towel and rub as much skin off the hazelnuts as will come off easily.

To toast whole spices and seeds: Spread the seeds in a dry skillet over medium heat and lightly toast them, stirring frequently, until fragrant. Pour the seeds into a pie pan or other flat dish to stop the cooking. This technique is commonly used for sesame, cumin, and coriander seed.

Crush seeds or whole spices in a mortar or, if you don't have one, corral the seeds on a cutting board and crush them with the flat side of a cleaver or a large French chef's knife. Or, you can put them in a small, not-too-flimsy plastic bag, close it, place it on a cutting board, and crush the seeds with a mallet or even a hammer.

Raw eggs, raw fish, and raw shellfish are not recommended for pregnant women, children, the elderly, or anyone with immune deficiencies. If you wish, in recipes using uncooked egg whites, such as Cranberry Semifreddo (page 218) and Roasted Rhubarb Honey Mousse (page 202), you can substitute a pasteurized egg white product, such as Just Whites or Eggology, for the fresh egg whites. With these products, you might need to beat a bit longer to get the whipped egg white volume you expect.

Nighttime in the South Granville Rise neighborhood, Vancouver, British Columbia

CHEFS' SECRETS: HOW CHEFS GET SO MUCH DONE, SO SMOOTHLY

Have you ever wondered how chefs make what they do look so easy? Well, sometimes it is easy and sometimes not. Good cooking has many facets: lots of practice and hard work, a true feel for cooking, and a few tried-and-true tricks of the trade. Every cook and chef has these special secrets up his or her sleeve, from a piece of equipment that makes life easier to a little procedure that is a smack-in-the-head, "Why didn't I think of that?" experience when you learn about it.

HOW DO CHEFS MAKE PUTTING OUT TWO HUNDRED DINNERS SEEM SO EFFORTLESS?

Mise en place: This French phrase means "put in place." It refers to the preparation chefs do to have everything ready and staged in advance so that the final cooking and presentation of a meal looks easy.

Begin with planning: Your menu should include a mix of easy dishes and more challenging ones; consider what equipment and which utensil you will use to cook each item. For instance, don't plan to bake rolls at the same time you've got a roast in the oven because they will probably need to be cooked at different temperatures. When serving appetizers, choose one item that's hot and a couple of cold ones.

Write out your menu: Next to each item, note the serving vessel or plate it's going on. Do you need a serving utensil? And what pieces of cutlery will be needed for the place setting? Then list for each course each component that's going on the plate, and star what needs to be prepped. Draw a diagram of each dish's presentation if it's complicated.

Write up a loose timeline of what to do when: Prepare "kits" for each item on the menu. The day of serving, create *mise en place* trays, and then, on your list, highlight each item as you tray it up. Use small dishes to hold cut herbs or tiny prepped items. It might be a bit more work ahead of time than you're used to, but it will give you a lot more time to spend with your guests. Since you have everything prepped, there will be no need to get stressed out!

WHAT MAKES THAT BEAUTIFUL GOLDEN CRUST ON THE CHICKEN SO CRISP AND THE INSIDE SO TENDER AND JUICY?

Finishing in the oven: If you find it a challenge to get several dishes ready to serve at the same time, this could be the tip you need. Many restaurant dishes are started on a stove-top burner—either sautéed or seared in a very hot pan—then transferred to a preheated oven to finish cooking. This gives the chef a few minutes to finish the sauce or other accompaniment for the dish and also gives the salmon steak or fillet, pork loin, or duck breast a nice "crust" with a juicy interior. Citrus Teriyaki Salmon with Pineapple Salsa (page 104) and Fan Tan Duck Breast with Blackberries (page 143) illustrate this technique.

Brining: This technique makes for moister meat and adds flavor as well. Grilled Chicken with Fresh Corn Salsa (page 161) uses a zingy chipotle chile brine.

WHAT MAKES THAT SAUCE SO RICH TASTING?

Reduction: This refers to evaporating sauces, stocks, and other liquids to concentrate their flavors. Use medium-high to high heat, and wait to add salt until after you've reduced—otherwise the food is likely to be oversalted. Fullers Five-Onion Soup (page 79), Spot Prawn Pasta with Lemon Cream (page 101), and Soy, Ginger & Sake Beef Pot Roast with Shiitakes (page 145) are good examples of this method.

AND WHAT MAKES THE PLATES AND PRESENTATIONS ALWAYS LOOK SO SPECIAL?

Favorite gadgets: *Chefs have a knack for breathtaking presentations that often utilize special cuts for vegetables. But you don't have to have professional knife skills to achieve spectacular looks for your dishes.*

Japanese mandoline: A heavy plastic frame that holds any one of several blades, as well as a guiding plate that can be adjusted according to the desired thickness of the cut. Many chefs prefer the Japanese mandoline over the French (metal) type because it's simpler to use, cheaper, and, most important, doesn't collapse on you at critical moments! My favorite model is Benriner, which can be used for making paper-thin cuts and hair-like, ultra-skinny vegetables. I recommend that you also purchase a metal mesh glove to protect your hand when using a mandoline. These cut-resistant gloves are available from restaurant supply and cutlery stores, Sur La Table (see page 223), and other kitchen shops.

Spiral cutter: This device, also available in shops that stock Asian cooking utensils, can turn raw vegetables into beautiful long, curly strands. Spiral-cut golden yellow and red beets make fabulous crunchy poufs to garnish a salad!

Squeeze bottles: These can be filled with brilliant sauces, oils, and reductions—an array of flavorful pigments to paint the plate with! Try getting creative with the Raspberry Drizzle on the Bittersweet Chocolate Bread Pudding (page 203), or have a little fun with chocolate sauce on the plates of your next chocolate dessert.

Microplane grater: This ultra-sharp tool is excellent for deftly minced citrus zest; just be careful not to grate into the white membrane under the colored rind. The implement can also be used for diaphanously fine gratings of hard cheese; creating a fine rain of cheese directly over pasta at the table is impressive.

Diamond Fingers knife sharpener: A sharp knife is the best tool you can have in the kitchen, and cooking is a lot more fun when you're not struggling to cut things up. Sharp knives are much less dangerous than dull ones because you can cut easily: the knife is doing the work; since you are not having to press down so hard, there's less chance for your knife to slip. I am not a huge fan of knife sharpeners, but the Diamond Fingers sharpener actually works great. After sharpening, I always finish the knife edge with a steel.

Some of these gadgets can be found at my online store, www.kathycasey.com, or at well-stocked kitchen and gourmet stores (see Sources, page 222).

SIPS AND STARTERS

Sunset Sage **Margarita**

MAKES 1 DRINK

The margarita goes high fashion with this elegant presentation. Fresh sage is a natural with the dusty flavor of tequila, and I recommend using a reposado tequila, such as El Tosoro, for this drink. Serve it with a big bowl of Sassy Watermelon Salsa (page 71) and fresh-made corn chips.

1 fresh sage leaf

1½ ounces tequila

½ ounce Cointreau, Triple Sec, or
    Grand Marnier

½ ounce cranberry juice cocktail

½ ounce Simple Syrup (recipe follows)

½ ounce fresh lime juice

Garnish
Fresh sage leaf

Crush the sage leaf and drop into a cocktail shaker. Fill the shaker with ice, then measure in the remaining liquid ingredients. Cap and shake vigorously until very cold.

Strain into a chilled cocktail glass and float a fresh sage leaf for garnish.

Simple Syrup

MAKES 8 CUPS

4 cups sugar

4 cups water

Combine the ingredients in a heavy saucepan. Bring to a boil, stirring to dissolve the sugar. Boil for 2 minutes. Remove from the heat and let cool. Bottle and store at room temperature until needed. Keeps indefinitely.

CHEF'S NOTE: Simple syrup is also available at bar supply stores.

Cucumber Sake **Martini**

MAKES 1 DRINK

If you are a sushi-lover, then you have to try this Asian-influenced martini. It is fantastic served with sushi or other Asian and Pacific Rim dishes or appetizers. The cucumber flavor comes through crisp and clean. For this recipe, a large, regular market cucumber will give more "cucumbery" flavor than the milder English variety.

3 slices cucumber

1½ ounces vodka

½ ounce premium sake

¾ ounce fresh lime juice

¾ ounce Simple Syrup (page 36)

Garnish

Thin slice of cucumber

Tear the cucumber slices in half and drop into a cocktail shaker. Fill the shaker with ice, then add the vodka, sake, lime juice, and simple syrup. Cap and shake vigorously until very cold.

Strain into a chilled cocktail glass. Garnish and serve immediately.

Raspberry Thyme **Fizz**

MAKES 1 DRINK

Waiter, there's thyme in my cocktail! That's right, fresh herbs have moved in to the bar and are welcome émigrés from the kitchen. Fresh thyme pairs marvelously with raspberry and sparkling wine. This drink is refreshing in the summer and also adds sparkle during the winter holidays; serve it as your signature cocktail at your next party.

1 fresh thyme sprig

¾ ounce Absolut Raspberri vodka

¾ ounce vodka

¾ ounce fresh lemon juice

1 ounce white cranberry juice drink

¾ ounce Simple Syrup (page 36)

Splash of Champagne or sparkling wine

Garnishes

Small fresh thyme sprig

Fresh raspberry (if in season)

Break the thyme sprig over a cocktail shaker, then drop it in and fill the shaker with ice. Measure in the vodkas, juices, and simple syrup. Cap the shaker and shake vigorously, at least 10 times, until very cold.

Strain into a cocktail glass and top with Champagne. Garnish with the thyme and raspberry.

CHEF'S NOTE: This cocktail is also delicious made with Finlandia mango vodka instead of raspberry vodka.

Oregon's raspberries fresh from the vine

Cherry Mojitos for a Crowd

Pick a scrumptious sweet cherry, such as Bing or Lambert, for this recipe. If you have a bumper crop of your own, you can always pit some cherries and freeze them for a taste of summer in the winter.

1 bunch fresh mint (about 1½ cups sprigs)

3 cups Bacardi Limón rum

2 cups sugar

2 cups fresh lime juice

¼ cup clear cherry liqueur, such as
    Maraska maraschino

3 cups pitted fresh sweet cherries
    (about 1½ pounds)

Loads of ice for serving

Two 10-ounce bottles soda water

Garnishes

Fresh mint sprigs

Fresh cherries on the stem

In a large nonreactive container, such as a glass pitcher, combine the mint, rum, sugar, lime juice, liqueur, and pitted cherries. Stir well to dissolve the sugar. Cover and refrigerate overnight.

For each serving, fill a large rocks glass or tumbler with ice and measure in 6 ounces (¾ cup) of the rum mixture (I like to use a ladle to do this), being sure to get some of the cherries into each glass. Top with 2 ounces (¼ cup) of soda. Stir, then garnish with a mint sprig and a cherry.

CHEF'S NOTE: You can make the cherry-rum mixture up to 3 days in advance and keep it refrigerated—the flavors will just get better and better.

Rainy Day **Manhattan**

MAKES 1 DRINK

This mingling of warming flavors will take the chill off even the grayest Northwest day.

2 ounces bourbon
½ ounce sweet (red) vermouth
½ ounce Frangelico liqueur
Dash of bitters

Garnish
Toasted unskinned hazelnut

Fill the cocktail shaker with ice, then measure in the bourbon, vermouth, and liqueur. Shake in the bitters. Cap and shake vigorously until very cold.

Strain into a chilled cocktail glass and float the hazelnut for garnish.

COCKTAIL BASICS

* Use lots of fresh ice and keep it drained well.

* Mix only high-quality ingredients— from liquors to mixers.

* Cut fresh garnishes not too far in advance.

* Rinse cocktail shakers or shaking tins after every drink.

* Prechill glasses by filling with ice and a splash of water.

* Cocktail-Making Measurements

    1 ounce = 2 tablespoons

    ¾ ounce = 1½ tablespoons

    ½ ounce = 1 tablespoon

    ¼ ounce = ½ tablespoon

Oregon Pear Side Car

MAKES 1 DRINK

Master mixologist Ryan Magarian, my senior beverage associate at Kathy Casey Food Studios, gives a classic Side Car this Northwest twist, in which he incorporates pear brandy from the Clear Creek Distillery in Portland, Oregon. The delectable eau-de-vie was created by Steve McCarthy to utilize his family's prolific Bartlett pear harvest.

⅛ orange or ¼ tangerine

Superfine sugar for rimming glass

1½ ounces vodka

½ ounce Clear Creek pear brandy

¾ ounce Simple Syrup (page 36)

¾ ounce fresh lemon juice

Pinch of ground cloves

Garnish
Paper-thin slice of pear

Rim a cocktail glass by first wiping the edge all around with the piece of orange, then dipping the rim into superfine sugar.

Squeeze and drop the citrus wedge into a cocktail shaker, then fill with ice. Measure in the vodka, brandy, simple syrup, and lemon juice. Cap the shaker and shake vigorously, at least 10 times.

Strain into the glass and dust the surface of the drink very lightly with cloves. Garnish with the pear slice.

Herbalicious

MAKES 1 DRINK

Nonalcoholic drinks should be just as special as those made with liquor. This sophisticated-tasting cocktail shakes in the fresh and herby flavors of mint and rosemary. I also like to serve this drink "up," that is, strained into a stemmed glass.

1 large fresh rosemary sprig

2 large fresh mint sprigs

1 large wedge pink grapefruit
   (about ⅛ grapefruit)

2 ounces peach or apricot nectar

1 ounce fresh lemon juice

1 ounce Simple Syrup (page 36)

Large splash of soda water

Garnish
Fresh rosemary sprig

Break up the herb sprigs over a cocktail shaker, then drop in. Squeeze the grapefruit wedge into the shaker, drop in, then fill with ice. Add the peach nectar and lemon juice and simple syrup. Cap the shaker and shake vigorously, at least 10 times, until very cold.

Pour into a rocks glass and top with soda. Garnish with the rosemary sprig.

Bloody Mary Deviled Eggs

MAKES 24 STUFFED EGGS

These aren't your ubiquitous party eggs! Inspired by their namesake cocktail, these are perfect to pair with a cold martini.

1 dozen eggs

¹⁄₂ cup mayonnaise or reduced-fat mayonnaise

¹⁄₂ teaspoon salt

1 tablespoon prepared horseradish

¹⁄₄ teaspoon celery seed

1 teaspoon Worcestershire sauce

¹⁄₂ teaspoon Tabasco sauce

Topping

¹⁄₂ cup ¹⁄₄ -inch-diced tomatoes

2 tablespoons minced celery

4 teaspoons minced pimiento-stuffed green olives

1 tablespoon fresh lemon juice

1 teaspoon vodka

Garnish

24 tiny celery-leaf sprigs (from the heart)

Put the eggs in a nonreactive saucepan and add cold water to 1 inch above the eggs. Bring to a boil over medium-high heat, then reduce the heat and simmer the eggs for 10 minutes. Remove from the heat and run cool water over the eggs in the pan until they are cooled. When cool, carefully peel them under running water.

Cut the eggs in half lengthwise and transfer the yolks to a bowl. Set the egg white halves on a platter, cover, and refrigerate.

With a fork or potato masher, mash the yolks to a smooth consistency. Mix in the mayonnaise, salt, horseradish, celery seed, Worcestershire, and Tabasco until smooth. (You can also do this in a mixing bowl with a whip attachment.)

Spoon the mixture into a pastry bag fitted with a plain or large star tip, then squeeze (pipe) the mixture evenly into the egg white halves.

To make the topping, mix the tomatoes, celery, olives, lemon juice, and vodka in a small bowl. Top each egg half with about 1 teaspoon of the mixture, then garnish each with a tiny celery sprig.

CHEF'S NOTE: You can boil the eggs up to 4 days in advance and refrigerate them. You can also peel and halve the eggs and make the filling 1 day ahead, and then assemble them up to 4 hours before serving, cover lightly with plastic wrap, and refrigerate. A piping bag and large star tip are of paramount handiness in deviled-egg making. You can purchase these tools at any well-stocked kitchen shop. Even better, in my view, than traditional pastry bags are the newer disposable piping bags. Just snip the end to fit your tip, fill and use, then remove the tip and toss away the messy bag—very convenient!

Chanterelle **Fritters**

A loose quantity of mushrooms is given for this recipe because, depending on the sizes and crevices of your mushrooms, you may need more or less of the buttermilk mixture and seasoned flour. Make more if needed. I like to squeeze a little fresh lemon juice over the fritters just before serving.

About 1 pound chanterelle mushrooms

Vegetable oil for frying

2 eggs

$\frac{1}{4}$ cup buttermilk

$\frac{1}{2}$ cup semolina

$\frac{1}{2}$ cup flour

$\frac{1}{4}$ cup cornmeal

$1\frac{1}{2}$ teaspoons salt

$\frac{1}{4}$ teaspoon black pepper

$\frac{1}{2}$ teaspoon paprika

$\frac{1}{4}$ teaspoon cayenne pepper

1 teaspoon very finely minced fresh thyme

1 teaspoon very finely minced fresh rosemary

Wipe or brush the chanterelles free of any dirt or pine needles and trim off any bad spots and the woody ends of the stems. Keep smaller chanterelles whole, and tear or cut the larger ones to halve or quarter. Set aside.

Meanwhile, in a deep fryer or Dutch oven, heat 4 inches of oil to 350°F.

In a small bowl, whisk the eggs and buttermilk. In a larger bowl, mix the remaining ingredients well.

Working in small batches, dip each mushroom into the flour mixture and then the egg mixture to coat well. Then put the mushroom back into the flour mixture, coating well again.

Immediately fry small batches of the mushrooms in the hot oil. Do not over-crowd the fryer. Move the fritters around with a spoon and turn as needed to get even cooking. Fry until golden and very crispy. Drain on paper towels and serve immediately.

Be sure to let the oil return to 350°F between batches of fritters.

HAZELNUTS

Ninety-nine percent of the U.S. hazelnut crop is produced in Oregon's Willamette Valley. The nuts mature during the summer, sheathed in their protective husks. After the nut is ripe, the husk releases it and drops it to the ground. Harvesting is usually in October, and the dusty business of hazelnut harvesting is something to be seen!

It starts with a mechanical operation, sweeping or blowing the nuts into long piles centered in the aisles between the rows of trees. Then a second machine vacuums up the nuts, and a large fan blows out the leaves and twigs. This procedure creates an actual dust storm in the field, and—let me tell you, I've been there—it's crazy! From the orchard, the fresh nuts are taken to a processing plant where they are washed, dried, and graded in the shell or cracked for marketing.

Hazelnuts come to us in several forms: whole, in the shell, to put out in big bowls to crack during the holidays; flour, or meal, to use in baking; hazelnut butter to spread on breakfast toast and top with raspberry jam; elegant oil to emulsify in salad dressings; and just good ol' shelled nuts. This flavorful nut is a staple of Northwest cookery.

Sweet & Spicy **Hazelnuts**

MAKES 3 CUPS

You'll find mixed spiced nuts and toasted hazelnuts set out for snacking at local brewpubs and alehouses. I like these nuts with a cold pint of lemony Hefeweizen.

1 pound hazelnuts (about 3 cups)
1 egg white
1 tablespoon water
⅓ cup sugar
¼ teaspoon ground cinnamon
¼ teaspoon ground nutmeg
2 teaspoons kosher salt
½ teaspoon cayenne pepper

Preheat an oven to 350°F. Spread the nuts on a large, rimmed baking sheet and bake for about 6 to 8 minutes or until they are lightly roasted and the skin is starting to come off. Remove from the oven and let cool. With a clean, non-fuzzy dish towel, rub the skins off the nuts. Reserve the baking sheet.

Meanwhile, reduce the oven heat to 250°F. In a medium bowl, whisk the egg white and water until foamy. Add the hazelnuts and toss to coat well. Transfer the nuts to a sieve, shake, and then drain for at least 2 minutes.

Mix all the remaining ingredients in a large bowl. Add the drained nuts and toss to coat thoroughly.

On the baking sheet, spread the nuts out in a single layer. Bake for 30 minutes. Stir with a spatula, spread the nuts out again, and bake 25 to 30 minutes longer, or until the nuts are dry.

Loosen the nuts from the baking sheet, then let them cool to room temperature on the sheet. Be sure to let the nuts cool completely and become crisp before putting them away. They can be stored for up to 1 month in an airtight container.

CHEF'S NOTE: These nuts are also lovely to package in pretty jars or decorative tins for holiday gifts.

Cheddar Ale Spread with Overnight Rosemary Semolina Flat Bread

MAKES 6 TO 8 SERVINGS

This recipe is total Oregon, known for its Tillamook Cheddar cheese, hazelnuts, and craft-brewed beers. Here, all three combine to make a full-bodied spread—just right to smear over crispy flat bread or crostini. Wash it all down with a cold one from Oregon, too, such as a Terminal Gravity IPA or a Deschutes Mirror Pond.

8 ounces cream cheese

2 teaspoons Dijon mustard

2½ cups (10 ounces) shredded extra-sharp Cheddar cheese, such as Tillamook

2 tablespoons half-and-half

¼ teaspoon Tabasco sauce

¼ teaspoon salt

¼ cup flavorful Northwest beer

2 tablespoons chopped fresh parsley

½ cup hazelnuts, lightly toasted, skinned (see page 30), and coarsely chopped (optional)

Overnight Rosemary Semolina Flat Bread (page 50), crackers, or crostini

Fresh rosemary sprigs for garnishing

Combine the cream cheese, mustard, Cheddar, half-and-half, Tabasco, and salt in a food processor. Process for about 30 seconds, add the beer, and continue processing until very smooth. Pulse in the parsley and hazelnuts until just dispersed.

Serve in a nice-looking container with the flat bread attractively broken up around it. Garnish with rosemary sprigs.

continued›

CHEF'S NOTE: You can keep the spread, refrigerated, for up to 4 days. Bring it to room temperature about 1 hour before serving.

Overnight Rosemary Semolina Flat Bread

MAKES 8 LARGE PIECES BEFORE BEING BROKEN UP

1 package active dry yeast (2¼ teaspoons)

1 teaspoon sugar

1 cup warm water (110°F), plus more if needed

2 tablespoons extra-virgin olive oil, plus more for drizzling

2½ cups flour, plus more for dusting

2 teaspoons very finely chopped fresh rosemary

½ cup semolina

1 teaspoon kosher salt, plus more for topping

In a large bowl, combine the yeast, sugar, and the 1 cup of water. Add the oil. Let sit for 10 minutes until foamy.

In a medium bowl, mix the flour, rosemary, semolina, and 1 teaspoon of salt.

Add the flour mixture to the yeast mixture, stirring with a large spoon to combine. Then, using clean hands and working in the bowl, mix until the dough comes together. If needed, add another 2 tablespoons warm water and continue mixing dough into a ball.

On a lightly floured surface, knead the dough for about 4 to 5 minutes.

Drizzle the bowl with ½ teaspoon oil and return the dough ball to the bowl, turning the dough to coat well with the oil. Cover the bowl with plastic wrap and refrigerate overnight or for up to 24 hours.

When ready to bake, preheat an oven to 425°F. Meanwhile, cut the dough into 8 wedges, then cover with a damp towel and let sit at room temperature for 10 to 15 minutes before rolling.

On a lightly floured surface, roll out each wedge into a 5-by-10-inch rectangle. Brush or drizzle with oil and sprinkle with salt to taste. Arrange on ungreased baking sheets and bake for 10 to 15 minutes until golden and crispy but not overbrowned.

CHEF'S NOTE: For even baking, rotate the pans in the oven and switch them from upper to lower racks midway through baking.

The Pacific Northwest is a paradise for the microbrew-lover. The brewmasters tout one-of-a-kind flavors from their catalogues of ongoing and seasonal offerings.

Seasonal beers give their makers creative freedom, allowing novel brews to be shaped based on agricultural availability and quaffers' changing palates. In summer, the Caldera Brewing Company of Ashland, Oregon, makes a light Lawnmower Lager, and at the 2005 Oregon Brewers Festival, Portland's Raccoon Lodge and Brewpub poured their Raspberry Wheat Beer. In the fall, Seattle's Elysian Brewery produces its Night Owl Pumpkin Ale, using 150 pounds of pumpkin in each batch, plus nutmeg, clove, cinnamon, ginger, and allspice. And silky Snowplow Milk Stout, with chocolate, coffee, and roasted malt essences, is a winter offering from Portland's Widmer Brothers Brewing Company.

The Northwest is the top producer of hops in the world, and 75 percent of the U.S. hops harvest comes from Washington's Yakima Valley. Northwest hops are sought after by the international brewing community, as 60 percent of the region's hop production goes overseas. More than seventeen varieties of the beer maker's "spice" of choice are cultivated here.

India pale ale (IPA) is the most widely brewed style of beer in the Northwest. An extra-strong and hoppy version of a pale ale, IPAs boast a strong hop nose, a light malt flavor, and an intensely bitter finish. The Northwesterner's gravitation to this hoppy style of beer gives our passion for bitter beer the name "hophead."

While Alaska and British Columbia have their share of local producers, the Greater Portland and Seattle areas are home to more breweries per capita than anywhere else in the United States. The best way to sample Northwest beer is either at the brewpub or at an alehouse with a loyal following. Many of the best brewpubs have only a few taps, but rotate the selection frequently, some daily.

The Northwest appreciation of craft-brewing excellence is manifested as locals and tourists alike tip back a cold one while enjoying some famous ale-battered halibut and chips, or after returning home when the day's work is done. You'd be hard-pressed to find a more refreshing and relaxing activity!

Pearl Balls with Ginger Soy Drizzle

MAKES ABOUT 32 BALLS

Chinese in origin, pearl balls are traditionally made with pork. For this number-one nibble, I've cut the pork with chicken breast to be a bit lighter but still full-flavored and bristling with "spiky" tender rice grains. When buying lemongrass, you usually have to purchase more than any one recipe calls for, so try keeping your extra lemongrass in the freezer. Just wrap the trimmed whole stalks and freeze. This also makes the herb tenderer and easier to chop (after defrosting).

2 cups Calrose rice

4 cups water

Meat Mixture

8 ounces boneless, skinless chicken breast, cut into 1/2-inch chunks

1 tablespoon minced shallot

2 teaspoons minced peeled fresh ginger

2 teaspoons minced fresh garlic

1 tablespoon very finely minced fresh lemongrass, white part only

2 tablespoons soy sauce

1 egg white, whisked

1/2 teaspoon salt

1/4 teaspoon red pepper flakes

8 ounces ground pork

1 green onion, finely sliced

Garnishes

Green onions, cut into fine diagonal slices

Ginger Soy Drizzle (facing page)

In a medium bowl, combine the rice and water. Cover and let soak for at least 2 hours or, refrigerated, overnight. When ready to make the pearl balls, drain the rice very well and set aside in a bowl.

To make the meat mixture, pulse the chicken in a food processor until chopped well but not "pasty"—the texture should be like ground meat. Add the shallot, ginger, garlic, lemongrass, soy sauce, egg white, salt, and pepper flakes and pulse until well mixed.

Transfer the mixture to a large bowl and, with clean hands, mix in the pork and green onion until well combined.

Portion and shape the mixture into scant-tablespoon-size balls (or use a No. 70 scoop), then drop each ball into the drained rice. Roll each ball in the rice to coat. (Discard any leftover rice.)

To cook the pearl balls, place the rice-studded balls, not touching, on a steamer rack or in a perforated pan or bamboo steamer. Set in a steamer or over boiling water, cover, and cook, maintaining the high steam, until the rice is tender and the meatballs are cooked through, about 15 minutes.

Transfer immediately to a serving platter. Skewer the pearl balls with picks and sprinkle with green onions for garnish. Serve the ginger soy drizzle on the side for dipping, or drizzle some over the balls.

CHEF'S NOTE: You can steam the pearl balls up to 1 day in advance and refrigerate. Reheat, covered, over steam or in the microwave (this works really well).

Ginger Soy Drizzle

MAKES ¾ CUP

1½ teaspoons vegetable oil

1 tablespoon minced fresh garlic

2 teaspoons minced peeled fresh ginger

1 tablespoon minced fresh lemongrass,
    white part only

¼ teaspoon red pepper flakes

3 tablespoons sugar

⅓ cup unseasoned rice vinegar

1 tablespoon water

⅓ cup soy sauce

In a small saucepan, heat the oil over medium heat and stir in the garlic, ginger, lemongrass, and pepper flakes. Cook, stirring, until the garlic and ginger are starting to become tender and get a little color, about 1 minute. (Be careful not to burn the garlic!) Stir in the sugar, then quickly add the vinegar, water, and soy sauce. Increase the heat to high and bring the sauce to a quick boil. Immediately remove from the heat and cool. Refrigerate until needed, for up to 1 week. Serve the sauce at room temperature.

Buddha in Seattle's International District

Traditional Native American salmon preparation

Salmon fishing is a true love of Northwest sportsmen and -women. The largest salmon caught in the Northwest was recorded in the 1930s in Petersburg, Alaska, weighing in at a whopping 128½ pounds. The thrill of reeling in a good fighter is the "big-one arm burn"; the good ache of your tired pole arm the next day is rewarded with a salmon barbecue with all the trimmings.

The early Native American tribes of the Northwest dined richly, the coastal waters serving up halibut, flounder, herring, and more. But the most important food to Northwest peoples was salmon. Called the "five tribes of salmon," the fish were denominated as they are today, the species being the pink, sockeye, king (chinook), chum, and silver (coho). Stories are told of rivers so thick with salmon you could walk across their backs.

Today, Alaska is the largest source of wild Pacific salmon, which is available fresh or frozen-at-sea. In Alaska, all five of the Pacific salmon species are fished sustainably, as certified by the Marine Stewardship Council.

Alaska's Copper and Yukon Rivers provide for the most highly desired salmon in May and June. These salmon have a long way to travel when they migrate from the ocean to their spawning grounds, so the fish must store a lot of fat to live on during their journey. That's why these are such super-fatty, moist, and flavorful fish.

I've cooked the iconic fish in many ways: grilled, broiled, barbecued, seared, and steamed, of course, and also baked in seaweed in a ground-dug pit heated with hot rocks. A traditional feature at Native American potlatch feasts was cedar-staked salmon, slow-roasted beside a driftwood fire. Cooked by radiant heat, the fish was moist and tender with a lightly smoked taste. This preparation is still enjoyed as the definitive method for cooking salmon. A close runner-up in my view is grilling over an open pit of alder coals, which impart a distinctive, woody perfume to the salmon's delicate flesh.

A true Northwest delight, salmon is also enjoyed in numerous other preparations, including pickled, cold-smoked, and hard-smoked. Native Americans brined then smoked the extra-rich salmon bellies, creating a candy-like sweet and salty hard-smoked piece of fish that could be eaten at a later time. Smoking salmon is still a favored way of preserving the catch of a lucky fisher.

Celebrated French chefs Gerard Parrat and Dominique Place left their respective Seattle restaurant posts to pursue their dream of smoking perfect, succulent salmon—and formed Gerard & Dominique Seafoods (see page 224) in 1989. One of the nation's best salmon smokeries, G&D ships to more than a hundred restaurants nationwide as well as to Japan. G&D Nova, Euro-style cold-smoked salmon, appears often on chefs' menus. It's delicious tucked under poached eggs for the supreme smoked-salmon Benedict. A holiday appetizer-table staple, with traditional condiments of capers and red onions served alongside, these days smoked salmon is also seen in the company of wasabi-spiked cream cheese and ginger pickled onions for a Pacific Rim twist.

Smoked Salmon & Little Cornmeal Pancake Bites

MAKES 24 PIECES

An appetizer party is not complete without some sort of smoked salmon. These pancake bites fit the bill, whether you top them with "hard" or hot-smoked or thin slices of lox or gravlax-style salmon. Most local sport fishermen/women do a hot-style smoke on their catch, using a soy-based brine, as in my grandfather Poppy's recipe. I also love the sliced European-style smoked salmon from Gerard & Dominique Seafoods and Port Chatham's Portlock lox-style smoked wild Copper River king.

Pancakes

½ cup water

½ cup plus ⅓ cup milk, plus more if needed

¼ cup fine-ground yellow cornmeal

½ cup flour

¾ teaspoon baking powder

¼ teaspoon salt

2 tablespoons butter, melted

1 egg, slightly beaten

2 tablespoons thinly sliced fresh chives

Vegetable oil for griddle (optional)

About ½ cup crème fraîche

4 to 6 ounces Poppy's Old-School Smoked Salmon (page 58) or other hot- or cold-smoked salmon

3 tablespoons thinly sliced fresh chives or coarsely chopped fresh dill for garnishing

CHEF'S NOTE: It is important to make sure the cornmeal is completely cooked. To test, take a small taste to be sure it is tender and doesn't have any crunch to it at all. And, if you have the patience to "stand facing the stove" that long, you can make the pancakes half-size, using only 1½ teaspoons batter for each, then adjusting the crème fraîche and salmon toppings accordingly.

To make the pancakes, combine the water and ½ cup of milk in a heavy, medium saucepan and bring to a simmer. Slowly sprinkle in the cornmeal, whisking constantly so that no lumps form. Simmer slowly, stirring frequently and adjusting the heat as necessary to prevent splattering, until the cornmeal is cooked and tender, about 4 minutes. Pour into a large bowl to cool to room temperature, stirring occasionally to prevent a skin from forming.

Meanwhile, sift the flour, baking powder, and salt together into a small bowl.

When the cornmeal mixture has cooled, whisk in the butter and egg, mixing until smooth. Stir in the flour mixture, then stir in ⅓ cup of milk. The batter should be fairly smooth and thick; if the batter is too thick, add milk, 1 teaspoon at a time. Fold in the chives.

Heat your favorite pancake pan over medium to medium-high heat, depending on the type of pan you are using. To test the pan's readiness, sprinkle with a few drops of water. If they "skittle around," the heat should be just about right. If needed, drizzle about 1 teaspoon or so of vegetable oil in the pan, then wipe with a paper towel to just lightly oil the surface and remove any extra grease.

For each pancake, drop 1 level tablespoon batter onto the heated griddle. Turn the pancakes when they are slightly puffy and a couple of bubbles have appeared on the surface. (These cakes have very few bubbles compared to regular pancakes.) The underside should be golden brown. Turn and cook until browned on the other side. The cooking time should be about 1 to 1½ minutes per side.

Cook the pancakes in batches, then top each one with about ¾ teaspoon crème fraîche, a small piece of salmon, and the herb garnish. (If you want to cook all the pancakes ahead, as each cake is done, put it on a wire rack. Reheat the pancakes, on the rack, lightly tented with foil, for about 5 minutes in a preheated 350°F oven before assembling.)

continued›

Poppy's Old-School Smoked Salmon

MAKES 2½ TO 3 POUNDS

My grandfather used to smoke salmon every year, as did almost every kid's dad, uncle, or grandpa who fished. This is my re-creation of his brine and method. This salmon is fabulous as is, whether as an entrée or a cocktail snack, or topping a salad, tossed with pasta, or folded into an omelet.

Brine

4 cups water

¼ cup kosher salt

½ cup packed light brown sugar

½ cup soy sauce

1 tablespoon granulated garlic

1 tablespoon pickling spices, crushed

4 pounds boneless, skinless wild salmon, cut into about 2-by-4-inch pieces

Apple wood chips

Whisk the brine ingredients in a 1-gallon or larger nonreactive container. Chill thoroughly.

Add the salmon, a few pieces at a time, to the brine, being sure that all sides of the fish have been bathed with brine and that the fish is completely immersed. (Weight the salmon down with a plate if necessary to keep it completely covered by the liquid.) Cover and refrigerate for at least 8 hours or overnight.

When ready to smoke the salmon, set up a smoker according to the manufacturer's instructions for hot-smoking the salmon without steam (dry). Fill the chip container with apple wood chips and preheat the smoker per the manufacturer's instructions until filled with smoke.

Meanwhile, spray the smoker racks with vegetable-oil cooking spray. Remove the fish from the brine and place the salmon pieces, spaced apart to allow good smoke circulation, on the racks. (Discard the brine.)

When the smoker is filled with smoke, add the racks and smoke the salmon until firm in thickest part and thoroughly cooked through, about 45 minutes to 1½ hours, depending on your smoker. About every 20 minutes during cooking, check the chip supply and replenish as needed to keep the smoker filled with smoke.

To test the salmon for doneness, cut a piece open; and as the smaller pieces are done, remove them from the smoker. When the salmon is done, serve immediately, or cool and refrigerate. Keeps, refrigerated, for up to 3 days or, frozen, for up to 1 month.

CHEF'S NOTE: The brine recipe makes about 5 cups, enough to brine 4 pounds of salmon. Be sure to discard the brine after use.

Cherry & Goat Cheese **Bings**

MAKES ABOUT 20 PIECES

Plump, juicy cherries, icy cold, are my idea of the perfect snack. Just sitting around on a hot day popping them in one by one is the start of a wonderful summer. But if you can keep from eating them all out of hand, fresh cherries can appear in any part of the menu, from beverages to baked goods and even, as here, appetizers. Named for my most adored variety of cherry, the big ambrosial Bing, this recipe is easy and requires very few ingredients. It's one of those recipes that are magically simple and delicious. I think a nice glass of chilled Northwest French-style dry "pink" wine, such as Barnard Griffin's Rosé of Shiraz, would be a peerless sipping partner.

20 fresh dark sweet cherries

½ cup (2 ounces) sliced almonds

1 teaspoon olive oil

Pinch of salt

4 to 6 ounces fresh goat cheese (chèvre)

Pit the cherries and set aside to drain on paper towels for 30 minutes.

Preheat an oven to 350°F.

Meanwhile, mix the almonds, oil, and salt in a small bowl, then spread on a rimmed baking sheet and bake for 5 minutes, or until golden brown. Let cool to room temperature. When cooled, use your hands to crush the almonds to the size of cracker crumbs; put into a shallow bowl.

Take 1 heaping teaspoonful of cheese in the palm of your hand, place a cherry on the cheese, and start rolling with your hands to coat the cherry. If there are any thin spots, add a bit more cheese. Immediately after rolling the cheese around the cherry, drop it into the crumbled almonds and roll to coat with the nuts. Repeat with the remaining cherries. Serve immediately, or refrigerate until ready to serve, for up to 2 hours.

OYSTERS

Clear, uncontaminated waters are key in growing top-quality oysters in the Pacific Northwest. The mollusks filter-feed gallons of water a day and gain their subtle, distinctive flavors from the environment they are grown in. Water temperature is also a factor, with the meat becoming firmer and tastier as temperature drops. Oysters are best eaten during the cold months when the waters are crisp. Northwest seafood "guru" Jon Rowley says, "You can tell it's oyster time in Seattle when the skies turn oyster gray—which is generally around the first of November."

In the early 1900s, seeds of *Crassostrea gigas,* commonly called Pacific oysters, were brought to the Northwest. This oyster loved the pristine waters, and Pacifics became the basis of the oyster industry. They are farmed in estuaries from southeastern Alaska to southern Oregon, and are known by their specific locales, such as Kachemak Bay (Alaska); Pendrell Sound, Fanny Bay, and Cortes Island (British Columbia); Hood Canal, Dabob, Quilcene, and Willapa Bays, Goose Point, Grays Harbor, Jorsted, Eagle, and Snow Creeks, Little Skookum and Totten Inlets, and Hamma Hamma River (Washington); and Yaquina, Netarts, and Coos Bays (Oregon).

The native Olympia oyster, *Ostrea lurida,* meanwhile, had some hard times. By the 1940s, it had become very scarce from pulp-mill pollution and overharvesting. Now, some years after the passage of the Clean Water Act and the hard work of oyster growers, Olympias are being farmed successfully in the southern Puget Sound and are even being reseeded in wild beds. These tiny toothsome bivalves are great for a first-time raw slurper and are ever so coveted by restaurants and their diners.

The largest producer of cultivated oysters, the Pacific Northwest grows more oyster species than anywhere else in the world. The species range in size from little Olympias to extra-large Pacifics, which are sometimes as big as tennis shoes. In between are the Kumamoto, or *Crassostrea sikamea,* a local favorite, and the European flat, or *Ostrea edulis.*

Small oysters are generally preferred for half-shell service, though true slurpers like a little "meat" on their oysters. The plump ones, with higher glycogen levels, are sweeter. Pacifics are routinely seen breaded, pan-fried, and served up with tartar sauce or as A.M. fare mingled in a Hangtown fry. On Asian menus, extra-large Pacifics are the choice for quickly steaming in the shell and splashing with salted black bean sauce. They are also a hit with the Hispanic market; the oysters are often barbecued, then streaked with smoky salsa and a squeeze of lime.

Traditionalists insist there is never a better way to eat oysters than raw "on the half shell," accompanied only with a crisp white wine and maybe a squirt of lemon. But which wines will pair with the salty-and-sweet, mineral, even metallic flavors in oysters? Good oyster wines are dry and clean-finishing, not fruity or oaky. You can confidently choose one of the winners of the annual Pacific Coast Oyster Wine Competition (see page 223).

Mountains of oyster shells at Willapa Bay

The region's oyster "culture" is celebrated in other ways, too. In October, the Skookum Rotary in Shelton stages the West Coast Oyster Shucking Championship and Washington State Seafood Festival, a.k.a. Oysterfest. This family-friendly event raises funds for numerous community organizations. The Oyster Cloyster Festival in Newport focuses on a competition among chefs to create the best oyster appetizers and benefits the Oregon Coast Community College Aquarium Science Program. The Clayoquot Oyster Festival in Tofino, British Columbia, includes tours of oyster farming on Lemmens Inlet and oysters cooked "everyway." And in Seattle, Anthony's Restaurant on Shilshole Bay sponsors the Oyster Olympics in March. Restaurant teams compete in oyster-shucking and oyster identification. Local notables get into the act, too, slurping oysters out of the half shell . . . with no hands allowed! (A few years back, I was the winner—slurping ten oysters in ten seconds!) It's all for a good cause, with proceeds going to the educational and cleanup programs of the nonprofit Puget Soundkeeper Alliance. The Pacific Northwest truly is an oyster-lover's paradise.

Oysters on the Half Shell with Champagne Mignonette Ice

MAKES ABOUT 2 CUPS ICE, ENOUGH TO TOP 5 TO 6 DOZEN OYSTERS

The pristine, unpolluted waters of Washington and British Columbia determine the distinguishing flavor charac-teristics of Northwest oysters and are a vital ingredient in producing the superior oysters that grow there. Purists say there is never a better way to eat raw oysters than unadorned, accompanied only with a squirt of lemon—and maybe not even that. But for "first-time users," sometimes a little "accessorizing" is needed and appreciated. The Champagne Mignonette Ice is my twist on mignonette sauce, a classic preparation of red wine vinegar, black pepper, and shallots. The simple, clean flavor complements but doesn't mask the oyster's essence.

Ice

3/4 teaspoon black peppercorns

1 cup Champagne vinegar

1/3 cup water

1 1/2 teaspoons very finely minced lemon zest

2 tablespoons minced shallot

1/2 cup dry Champagne

Northwest oysters such as Kumamotos
    or Pacifics, in the shell

Crushed ice for oyster platter

Prepare the mignonette ice the day before or up to 3 days in advance. Enclose the peppercorns between pieces of plastic wrap and crush well with a heavy pot or mallet (or use a mortar and pestle). In an 8-inch square freezerproof glass casserole dish or stainless-steel bowl, combine the pepper with the remaining ice ingredients and stir. Cover with plastic wrap and place in the freezer. Every 30 minutes or so, remove from the freezer and stir the mixture with a fork. The mixture should start becoming slushy after about 1 1/2 to 2 hours. When the mixture is icy and completely raked into tiny ice crystals, you can stop the stirring process. Let the mixture freeze overnight, then break up the ice crystals with a fork right before serving.

Wash the oysters, scrubbing the shells with a vegetable brush to remove any debris. Refrigerate until ready to shuck.

Right before serving, shuck the oysters, discarding the top shells. Inspect the oysters for any bits of broken shell, picking out carefully.

Serve the oysters on a platter of crushed ice. Serve the mignonette ice in a small bowl; guests can spoon a small spoonful over the oysters.

Roasted Figs with Gorgonzola & Walnuts

MAKES ABOUT 24 TO 30 PIECES

A lot of people—even locals—are surprised to hear that figs grow abundantly in the Northwest. Once you plant a tree and it starts producing, look out! You might have more than you know what to do with . . . but here's your answer. You won't believe that three ingredients can make such an extraordinary appetizer.

4 ounces Gorgonzola cheese

¼ cup chopped walnuts

1 pint fresh figs, halved lengthwise

Preheat an oven to 425°F. In a small bowl, mix the Gorgonzola and walnuts. Arrange the figs, cut-side up, on an ungreased baking sheet, and top each piece with 1 generous teaspoon of the Gorgonzola mixture.

Roast the figs for about 6 to 8 minutes, or until heated through and the cheese is hot. Let cool slightly and enjoy!

Tasty Dungeness Crab Cakes with Poufs of Slaw & Sherry Aioli

MAKES 24 CAKES

There are definitely crab-cake wars going on 24/7—it's the West Coast versus the East Coast. Who has the sweetest crab? Who's got the best crab cake? Who uses the least breading? On the West Coast, we are certainly prejudiced toward our sweet Dungeness crab, simply prepared—you'll find no Old Bay in these babies. But if Dungeness is unavailable, blue crab will do just fine.

Crab Mixture

1 pound fresh Dungeness crabmeat, drained well, or substitute lump crabmeat

1/3 cup mayonnaise

1 egg, lightly beaten

1 teaspoon Worcestershire sauce

1/2 teaspoon Tabasco sauce

3 tablespoons finely diced celery

3 tablespoons minced green onion

2 teaspoons minced fresh garlic

1/4 cup panko (Japanese bread crumbs) or fine dried bread crumbs

2 teaspoons fresh lemon juice

1/2 teaspoon kosher salt

1/8 teaspoon black pepper

2 tablespoons minced carrot

1 tablespoon chopped fresh parsley

2 eggs

2 teaspoons water

1 1/2 cups panko (Japanese bread crumbs) or fine dried bread crumbs

3 cups peanut or vegetable oil or as needed for frying

Tangy Vegetable Slaw (facing page)

Sherry Aioli (facing page)

2 lemons, cut into wedges, for garnishing

To make the crab mixture, mix all the ingredients in a large bowl. Divide by heaping tablespoonfuls into 24 portions, then form into 1/2-inch-thick patties.

Beat the eggs with the water in a small bowl. Put the panko in a separate bowl. Dip the patties in the egg wash, turning to coat. Shake off any excess, then dip in the panko, turning to coat evenly. (Be sure your cakes are nicely compact and pressed together.)

In a heavy, medium skillet or deep fryer, heat the oil over medium-high heat until hot but not smoking (350° to 375°F). Fry the cakes in batches, about 6 to 8 at a time, until golden brown on each side, turning as needed. The total cooking time should be about 2 to 3 minutes. Drain on paper towels.

Serve immediately, topping each cake with a pouf of slaw and a dollop of sherry aioli. Accompany with extra aioli and lemon wedges on the side.

Tangy Vegetable Slaw

MAKES 1½ CUPS

1½ tablespoons mayonnaise
1 tablespoon sour cream
2 tablespoons sugar
2½ tablespoons sherry vinegar
½ teaspoon kosher salt
⅛ teaspoon black pepper
¾ cup very finely shredded green cabbage
¼ cup very finely shredded red cabbage
½ cup finely julienned carrots
½ cup finely julienned unpeeled English
   cucumber
3 tablespoons ½-inch-long pieces
   fresh chives

In a large bowl, mix the mayonnaise, sour cream, and sugar. Whisk in the vinegar, salt, and pepper. Just before serving, add the remaining ingredients and toss well.

CHEF'S NOTE: You can prepare the dressing and vegetables for the slaw up to 2 days in advance and refrigerate separately. Toss them together right before serving.

Sherry Aioli

MAKES 1¼ CUPS

¾ cup mayonnaise
1 tablespoon minced fresh garlic
1½ teaspoons sherry vinegar
1½ tablespoons fresh lemon juice
½ cup extra-virgin olive oil
⅛ teaspoon Tabasco sauce
½ teaspoon kosher salt

In a medium bowl or in a food processor, combine the mayonnaise, garlic, vinegar, and lemon juice. While whisking vigorously or with the machine running, slowly drizzle in the oil until all of it is incorporated and the aioli is smooth.

Season with the Tabasco and salt, mixing well. Store refrigerated until needed, for up to 4 days.

Sesame Roasted Shrimp Sticks with Zippy Apricot Dipping Sauce

MAKES 16 TO 20 PIECES

With its mixture (usually) of fennel, cloves, cinnamon, star anise, and peppercorns, Chinese five-spice powder lends a complex and aromatic flavor profile. Some versions even contain seven ingredients, which might include ginger and nutmeg. Purchase the blend at an Asian market or from a spice merchant, such as Seattle Spice Czar Tony Hill's World Spice Merchants. And if you are heading to an Asian market, pick up some fresh shiso leaves to serve the shrimp on for a striking presentation.

Sauce

1 tablespoon dry English mustard, or more
    if you want it extra-zippy
1 tablespoon water
¾ cup apricot jam
1 tablespoon minced peeled fresh ginger
1 large or 2 small green onions, very thinly
    sliced
2 tablespoons unseasoned rice vinegar

Shrimp

1 egg white
½ teaspoon salt
½ teaspoon Chinese five-spice powder
1 tablespoon Asian sesame oil
2½ to 3 tablespoons sesame seed (I like
    to use a mixture of 3 parts white and
    1 part black seeds)
1 pound large shrimp (16 to 20)
16 to 20 four- to six-inch bamboo skewers,
    soaked in water for one hour

Make the sauce first, up to 3 days ahead. In a small bowl, mix the mustard and water and let sit for 5 minutes. Stir in the remaining ingredients until well mixed. If made ahead, refrigerate the sauce until shortly before serving. Serve the sauce warmed or at room temperature.

To prepare the shrimp, preheat an oven to 475°F. In a medium bowl, whisk the egg white, salt, five-spice, and oil. Put the sesame seed in a small bowl. Lightly oil a baking sheet or spray with vegetable-oil cooking spray. Peel, devein, and remove tails from the shrimp. Drop the shrimp into the egg white mixture and toss to coat thoroughly.

Skewer a shrimp, curled into a circle, on the tip of a skewer, so that it looks like a shrimp "lollipop." (Be sure to thread both head and tail ends of shrimp onto the skewer.) Sprinkle each side of shrimp with sesame seed. Repeat with the remaining shrimp. As each skewer is done, lay it on the baking sheet, spacing the skewers apart, not touching.

Roast the shrimp for about 5 minutes, or until just cooked through and pink.

Serve the shrimp skewers on a platter and the sauce in a small bowl with a tiny spoon for drizzling, or plate them with a small puddle of sauce.

Chicken Liver Pâté with Brandied Fruit & Sage Toast

MAKES 6 TO 10 SERVINGS

Dried fruits give a nice counterbalance to the savory liver. Serve this with a glass of Northwest bubbly, such as Domaine Ste. Michelle's Cuvee Brut.

Pâté

⅓ cup finely chopped dried fruit, such as apricots, peaches, or tart cherries

¼ cup Cognac or other brandy

4 tablespoons (½ stick) butter

¾ cup finely chopped onion

1 tablespoon minced fresh garlic

1 pound chicken livers, trimmed and drained well

1½ teaspoons kosher salt

¼ teaspoon ground allspice

¼ teaspoon black pepper

Toast

¼ cup olive oil

1 tablespoon minced fresh sage

24 slices baguette or other French bread

½ teaspoon kosher salt

Garnish

Fresh sage leaves

To make the pâté, in a small bowl, soak the dried fruit in the brandy, covered, overnight at room temperature. Drain the fruit, pressing out the brandy, and reserve the fruit and brandy separately.

In a large sauté pan or skillet, melt the butter over medium-high heat. Cook the onion, stirring often, for about 3 minutes, or until translucent. Add the garlic and cook for 30 seconds, then add the livers and sprinkle with the salt, allspice, and pepper. Cook for about 2 minutes, turning the livers as needed. Add the reserved brandy and increase the heat to high. Cook until the livers are still a bit pink on the inside and the brandy has cooked down until almost dry, about 1½ to 2 minutes.

Immediately transfer the mixture to a food processor. Process until smooth, then add the reserved fruit and pulse in just to mix, not to chop the fruit.

Pack the pâté into a 2-cup crock or pâté mold. Cover with plastic wrap pressed directly onto the surface and refrigerate for at least 4 hours or up to 3 days before serving.

To make the toast, preheat heat an oven to 375°F. Heat the oil and sage in a small saucepan over low heat until just warmed. Remove from the heat and let sit for 5 to 10 minutes to infuse the sage flavor.

Lay the baguette slices on a baking sheet and lightly brush them with the infused oil. Sprinkle with the salt, then bake for about 10 minutes, or until crisp.

Serve the pâté with the toasts around it, garnishing the platter with sage leaves.

Thai Chicken Lettuce Cups with Pineapple Nuoc Cham

MAKES 8 TO 12 APPETIZER SERVINGS

Laotian, Cambodian, Vietnamese, and Thai immigrants have introduced us to the foods of Southeast Asia, and nuoc cham, served at many Thai restaurants, has become a familiar table condiment. The characteristic flavor of this spicy sweet-and-salty dipping sauce comes from fish sauce, whose use, like soy sauce in Chinese cooking, adds a rounded, salty essence to savory dishes.

Nuoc Cham

2 tablespoons fish sauce

1 tablespoon sugar

½ to 1 teaspoon sambal oelek

1 teaspoon minced fresh garlic

2 tablespoons fresh lime juice

2 tablespoons unseasoned rice vinegar

½ cup chopped ripe fresh pineapple

Chicken Filling

1 tablespoon canola or other vegetable oil

1 pound ground chicken meat

1 tablespoon minced fresh garlic

1 tablespoon minced peeled fresh ginger

1 tablespoon minced fresh lemongrass

¼ cup thinly sliced green onion

1 tablespoon fresh lime juice

1 teaspoon salt

1 tablespoon fish sauce

Garnishes

½ cup fresh bean sprouts

½ bunch fresh cilantro

1 small bunch fresh Thai basil

1 small bunch fresh mint

Leaves from 1 large head butter lettuce, rinsed and spun dry

Lime wedges

½ English cucumber, halved lengthwise, then cut into thin diagonal slices

½ cup coarsely chopped dry-roasted salted peanuts

To make the nuoc cham, combine all the ingredients in a food processor and pulse until the pineapple is chopped well but not puréed. Set aside, or refrigerate for up to 2 days.

To make the chicken filling, heat a large nonstick skillet or sauté pan over medium-high heat until hot. Add the oil and heat until hot but not smoking, then add the chicken and cook, crumbling with a spoon, until almost done, about 4 minutes. Stir in the garlic, ginger, and lemongrass. Cook for about 1 minute more—do not brown the garlic. Stir in the green onion, lime juice, salt, and fish sauce and remove from the heat.

Serve the nuoc cham in a small bowl with a spoon, and the chicken in a medium bowl with a spoon. Rinse, dry, and pick over the bean sprouts and fresh herbs, breaking the herbs into nice, whole sprigs. Arrange the sprouts and herb sprigs in neat, separate piles on a large serving platter. Place the lettuce leaves in a separate pile on the platter, then garnish with lime wedges. Tuck in small bowls of cucumber and peanuts.

To assemble the lettuce cups, instruct your guests to take a lettuce leaf, mound with 2 to 3 tablespoons of chicken, garnish with cucumber slices, bean sprouts, and herbs, then sprinkle with peanuts. Drizzle with nuoc cham and season with additional squeezes of lime, if desired.

Beautiful local watermelon

Sassy **Watermelon Salsa**

MAKES 4 CUPS

Watermelon and other exotic sweet melons are grown in the eastern parts of Oregon and Washington, where the temperatures sometimes reach to 115°F plus. Hermiston, Oregon, located near the Blue Mountains, is known for its heat-collecting sandy soil, which helps create sugar in their coveted watermelons. Serve this salsa with lightly salted crispy tortilla chips for scooping.

2 tablespoons sugar

¼ cup fresh lime juice

¼ cup finely diced sweet white onion

4 cups ¼-inch-chopped seeded watermelon

¼ cup chopped fresh cilantro

2 tablespoons minced seeded fresh jalapeño chile, or to taste

1 teaspoon coriander seed, lightly toasted, then crushed (see page 30)

In a large bowl, dissolve the sugar in the lime juice. Gently toss in the remaining ingredients. Serve immediately.

CHEF'S NOTE: You can prepare the components up to 2 hours in advance, refrigerate them separately, and toss them together right before serving.

SOUPS AND SALADS

Palouse Lentil & Sausage Soup

MAKES ABOUT 12 CUPS, OR 6 TO 12 SERVINGS

Washington state ranks No. 1 in national lentil production. The legumes are grown in the Palouse, a scenic expanse of wind-formed rolling hills named for the Native American tribe. The region is centered around Pullman, Washington, and features hundred-foot-deep topsoil rich with volcanic ash. High in iron, protein, and soluble fiber, lentils are not only good for you but great-tasting—especially in soups.

2 tablespoons olive oil

8 ounces hot Italian sausage, bulk or
   removed from casings

1 cup chopped onion

3/4 cup chopped celery

3/4 cup chopped carrot

1 teaspoon ground cumin

1/4 teaspoon ground cinnamon

1/2 teaspoon black pepper

1/2 teaspoon smoked Spanish paprika
   (pimentón)

1/2 teaspoon dried thyme leaves

1 bay leaf

1 tablespoon minced fresh garlic

2 cans (14 1/2 ounces each) diced peeled
   tomatoes

2 cups brown lentils, rinsed and picked over

6 cups low-sodium chicken broth or
   homemade chicken stock

2 cups water

1 tablespoon sherry vinegar

Salt

In a large, heavy soup pot or Dutch oven, heat the oil over medium-high heat and sauté the sausage, breaking it up thoroughly, for 3 to 4 minutes, or until about halfway cooked. Stir in the onion, celery, and carrot and sauté until sausage is browned and vegetables are tender. Add the spices, thyme, bay leaf, and garlic and sauté for about 1 minute more.

Stir in the tomatoes, lentils, broth, and water and bring to a boil, then reduce the heat to low and simmer, stirring frequently, until lentils are tender, about 20 to 30 minutes. If the soup becomes too thick during cooking, add a little more water. Stir in the vinegar and season to taste with salt. Remove the bay leaf before serving.

CHEF'S NOTE: This hearty soup makes a warming fall or winter light supper when paired with crusty bread and a big glass of red wine. You can make the soup up to 3 days in advance; it is actually even better when served the next day after cooking.

Roasted Beet Soup with Coriander

MAKES 6 TO 8 APPETIZER OR 4 ENTRÉE SERVINGS

Homemade pickled beets were a real treat as a Sunday-dinner accompaniment back when everyone's mom or grandmother canned. Today, beets, fresh from the farmers' markets, are served in many more "modern" preparations. This brilliant pink soup—made with beets slow-roasted to bring out their sweetness—will turn the most resistant beet-eater into a beet-lover.

1½ pounds beets (without leaves), tops trimmed to 2 inches

3 tablespoons butter

½ cup chopped onion

1 tablespoon minced fresh garlic

2 teaspoons coriander seed, lightly toasted and ground or crushed (see page 30)

¼ teaspoon red pepper flakes

3 cups low-sodium chicken broth or homemade chicken stock

½ cup sour cream

2 tablespoons fresh lime juice

3 tablespoons chopped fresh cilantro

Salt

Garnishes

Sour cream thinned with a little water

Chopped fresh cilantro

Lime wedges

Wash the beets, leaving the roots untrimmed. Put the beets in a baking pan, cover with foil, and poke 6 holes in the foil. Roast the beets in a 375°F oven until very tender, allowing about 2 hours or more.

When the beets are thoroughly tender, remove from the oven, and as soon as they are cool enough to handle, slip the skins off and cut beets into large chunks. (You can do this part the day before, if necessary.)

In a large soup pot or Dutch oven, heat the butter over medium-high heat and sauté the onion for about 3 minutes, or until translucent. Add the garlic, coriander seed, and pepper flakes and cook, stirring, for about 1 minute. Add the broth and beets and cook until beets are heated through.

Working in small batches, purée the soup with the sour cream in a food processor or blender until smooth. Return the puréed soup to the pan and heat until hot, but do not boil. Right before serving, whisk in the lime juice and cilantro and season with salt to taste.

For a fun garnish, swizzle the top of the soup with a little thinned-out sour cream and a sprinkling of cilantro. Pass lime wedges for squeezing into the soup.

CHEF'S NOTE: You can make this soup vegetarian by substituting full-flavored vegetable broth for the chicken broth.

Sunnyside **Asparagus Soup** with Orange Cream & Poppy Seed Crackers

MAKES 8 TO 10 APPETIZER OR 6 ENTRÉE SERVINGS

Sunnyside is a small town tucked among wineries in Eastern Washington, where I have had some of the tastiest Northwest asparagus ever. "Grass" is a toughie to pair with wine—but not when you're eating asparagus with a wine maker! I have relished many a spear with Chinook Winery owners Kay Simon and Clay Mackie while sipping a glass of their semillon—a food and wine match some say can never happen.

2 pounds asparagus, bottom 2 inches
    trimmed off

3 tablespoons olive oil

1/2 cup chopped onion

2 large shallots, chopped

2 teaspoons minced fresh garlic

2 teaspoons minced orange zest

1 cup 1-inch-diced russet potatoes

5 cups low-sodium chicken broth or
    homemade chicken stock

4 fresh mint leaves (optional)

1 cup heavy whipping cream

Salt

Freshly ground white pepper

Orange Cream

1 tablespoon minced orange zest

1/2 cup heavy whipping cream

1/8 teaspoon salt

Poppy Seed Crackers (page 78)
    for serving

Wash the asparagus well, then cut into 1-inch pieces. Set aside.

Heat the oil in a large saucepan over medium heat, and cook the onion and shallots over medium heat until the onion is translucent, about 5 to 7 minutes. Add the garlic, zest, potatoes, and broth and bring just to a boil. Reduce the heat and simmer for 10 minutes, then add the asparagus, return to a simmer, and cook for about 5 minutes more, or until just tender.

In a food processor or blender, purée the soup in batches, with the mint if using, until smooth. Return the soup to the pan, add the cream, and heat until hot. Season to taste with salt and pepper.

Meanwhile, in a small bowl, whip the orange cream ingredients together until just softly peaked.

Ladle the soup into bowls, then dollop with the cream. Accompany with the crackers.

Continued›

CHEF'S NOTE: A lot of people say they prefer the tiny, wispy asparagus spears, but I don't think they have the big flavor of larger stalks. I prefer them fat-finger-thick. This soup can also be served cold.

Poppy Seed Crackers

MAKES ABOUT 32 PIECES

1 cup flour

$^1\!/_2$ teaspoon salt

1 teaspoon sugar

1 tablespoon butter, cut into small pieces

2 tablespoons poppy seed

4 to 6 tablespoons milk

Kosher salt for sprinkling

In a food processor, combine the flour, salt, sugar, butter, and 1 tablespoon of the poppy seed. Pulse until the mixture resembles a coarse meal. With the machine running, gradually add 4 tablespoons of milk, then, if the dough is dry, add more, 1 tablespoon at a time. Process until the dough comes together. Transfer the dough to a piece of plastic wrap and wrap well. Let rest for at least 30 minutes or up to 1 hour before proceeding.

Preheat an oven to 350°F. Transfer the dough to a lightly floured surface and divide into 8 pieces. Press each piece into a disk to fit a pasta machine. Run the dough through the machine several times, each time reducing to a thinner setting. Do this until the dough is cracker-thin (about $^1\!/_8$ inch thick). The dough can also be hand-rolled—it just takes some muscle! If hand-rolling, roll the dough into long, rectangular pieces.

Place the rolled-out pieces on large baking sheets lined with parchment paper and lightly mist or brush the dough with water. Sprinkle with kosher salt and the remaining 1 tablespoon poppy seed, pressing them in a bit with your hand if needed. Using a fork, prick the dough all over.

Bake for 10 to 15 minutes, or until the crackers are lightly browned and crisp. Let cool. Break each cracker into about 4 pieces. Serve immediately, or store in a tightly covered container for up to 1 week.

Fullers **Five-Onion Soup**

MAKES ABOUT 10 SERVINGS

This soup is from the former Seattle restaurant Fullers, where I was executive chef during the rise of Northwest cuisine in the eighties. The item was, as we say in the restaurant business, a "sacred cow," meaning there would be throngs of protesters if you ever took it off the menu. The wonderfully rich soup takes quite awhile to reduce to its caramelized goodness but is worth the time invested.

2 large leeks

1 medium red onion, cut into large chunks

1 medium yellow onion, cut into large chunks

1 medium white onion, cut into large chunks

4 shallots

6 cloves fresh garlic

4 tablespoons (½ stick) butter

1 cup dry sherry

1 bay leaf

6 black peppercorns, crushed

1 tablespoon chopped fresh thyme, or
    1 teaspoon dried

6 cups low-sodium chicken broth or
    homemade chicken stock

3 cups heavy whipping cream

¼ cup brandy

1 tablespoon cornstarch

¼ teaspoon white pepper

Salt

Thinly sliced fresh chives for garnishing

Coarsely chop the leeks, discarding the tough green parts, and rinse them well to remove sand.

In two batches, process the leeks, onions, shallots, and garlic in a food processor until finely chopped but not mushy. (Do not overprocess.)

Melt the butter in a large, heavy Dutch oven or soup pot over medium heat. Slowly sauté the onions for 12 to 15 minutes, stirring often, until they just turn a bit golden. Stir in the sherry, scraping up any browned bits in the pan. Add the bay leaf, peppercorns, thyme, and broth. Bring to a simmer, reduce the heat to medium to medium-low, and simmer for 1 hour, or until golden in color and rich in flavor. Add the cream and simmer the soup another 30 minutes.

Mix the brandy and cornstarch and whisk into the simmering soup. Add the white pepper, then season with salt to taste. (The amount of salt needed will vary, depending on whether you used homemade stock or canned broth.) Simmer for 3 to 4 more minutes. Remove the bay leaf.

Serve immediately, garnished with chives.

Strawberry & Spinach Salad with Sweet Onions and Poppy Seed–Ginger Vinaigrette

MAKES 6 TO 8 SERVINGS

Intensely sweet and juicy Northwest strawberries are available for only a few weeks each year and are highly perishable due to their high sugar content. But when they are in season, you'll want to make this salad!

Vinaigrette

¼ cup white wine vinegar

1 tablespoon minced peeled fresh ginger

2 tablespoons Dijon mustard

3 tablespoons honey

2 tablespoons sugar

½ teaspoon salt

¼ teaspoon black pepper

⅓ cup light olive oil or other salad oil

2 teaspoons poppy seed

Salad

3 cups fresh strawberries, stemmed and
  quartered, or another local berry, such as
  raspberries, blackberries, or blueberries

2 bunches spinach, stemmed, washed well,
  and spun dry (8 to 10 cups)

½ cup thinly sliced sweet white onion,
  such as a Walla Walla Sweet

½ cup sliced almonds, toasted (see page 30)

To make the vinaigrette, whisk the vinegar, ginger, mustard, honey, sugar, salt, and pepper in a medium bowl. Gradually whisk in the oil, emulsifying the vinaigrette. Stir in the poppy seed. Refrigerate for up to 2 days.

To make the salad, toss the berries, spinach, and onion with the vinaigrette. Sprinkle with almonds.

CHEF'S NOTE: You can substitute toasted hazelnuts for the almonds. This salad is also excellent as an entrée salad, topped with grilled chicken cut into strips.

CRAB

The Northwest definitely has its share of crabs—from the beloved Dungeness crab to the Alaskan king crab, the snow crab, and the red rock crab.

Named for a Washington town on the Strait of Juan de Fuca, the Dungeness crab is found all the way from Alaska to lower California. Its scientific name, *Cancer magister,* means "big crab." This sweet crustacean has always been a seaside treat. The best, truly Northwest way to enjoy it is to cook it live right on the beach in a pot of boiling seawater. Then sit down right there in the sand and start cracking while breathing in the fresh sea air. Dip the luscious meat in melted butter and squeeze a little lemon on it, or dip it in mayonnaise that has been mixed with a little chili sauce or cocktail sauce. Accompany simply, and wash it all down with a glass of cold crisp Northwest semillon. All of a sudden you haven't a care in the world but just to sit and crack crab.

Fresh and right out of the shell might still be a favorite way to eat this much-praised Northwest creature, but no one turns it down any way they can get it! Since Dungeness are most bountiful during the winter, it's a good time to eat crab in a second favorite form, crab cakes. Crab cakes are an American institution; from Chesapeake Bay to Puget Sound, each region has its version. Northwest foodies and chefs are opinionated about their crab cakes, sometimes even downright crabby! Locally, you find crab cakes in a multitude of styles with accompaniments ranging from conventional tartar sauce to sweet-roasted-pepper coulis to Pacific Rim–influenced lemongrass or ginger aioli. Some swear by Dijon mustard as their secret ingredient; others say milk-soaked bread crumbs or mayonnaise does the trick for moistness. But few will argue that high-quality crabmeat, preferably fresh rather than frozen . . . and lots of it, is the best secret ingredient.

King crab typically comes to us in the form of cooked giant legs. They are usually cracked and eaten cold with melted butter—yum! Traditionally, "crab feeds" have been crowd-pleasing fundraisers for Northwest politicians and civic groups, and many people have fond memories of these feasts. My best crab memory of all is from a charity-auction dinner that I cooked with Julia Child at a Seattle home. The lucky bidders flew in a live king crab, which we cooked outside in a giant pot then ate warm, simply dipped in butter with a little squeeze of lemon. And this was just the appetizer to start a fantastic Northwest meal. Julia definitely said, *"Bon appetit!"*

Classic Seattle-Style **Crab Louis**

MAKES 4 SERVINGS

Seattleites uniformly say that the original Crab Louis was invented by a chef at the grand old Olympic Hotel in Seattle, now the Fairmont Olympic Hotel. But what there's definite dispute over is the dressing ingredients—whether it should have hard-cooked eggs in it, or sweet pickle relish, or chopped black olives. My version has them all! Though this salad is traditionally made with sweet Dungeness crabmeat, many restaurants and Louis-lovers also add a mound of sweet Oregon bay shrimp, a Northwest salad staple.

4 large whole lettuce leaves

8 heaping cups sliced iceberg or
   romaine lettuce

1 pound Dungeness crab body and leg meat

4 hard-boiled eggs, halved lengthwise

12 grape tomatoes

12 cooked asparagus spears and/or raw
   cucumber slices

12 black ripe olives

4 lemon wedges

4 flat-leaf parsley sprigs

Louis Dressing (recipe follows)

Lay 1 whole lettuce leaf on each chilled individual plate. Divide the cut lettuce among the leaves and top with the crabmeat. Divide the eggs, tomatoes, asparagus, and olives attractively among the salads.

Garnish with lemon wedges and parsley sprigs. Serve about 1/3 cup of dressing in a large ramekin with each salad and pass extra dressing.

Louis Dressing

MAKES 2 3/4 CUPS

Classic uses of this dressing include Crab or Shrimp Louis and the again-hip retro "wedge" of iceberg lettuce salad. You can use it instead of Russian dressing on Reuben sandwiches. And it's a Northwest institution as a dip for cracked crab.

2 hard-boiled eggs, very finely chopped

1/3 cup chopped black ripe olives

3 tablespoons fresh lemon juice

1 1/2 cups mayonnaise

1/2 cup tomato-based chili sauce

1/4 teaspoon black pepper

1/2 teaspoon Tabasco sauce or to taste

1 teaspoon Worcestershire sauce

1/3 cup sweet pickle relish

1 tablespoon minced white onion

In a medium bowl, mix all the ingredients well. The dressing keeps, refrigerated, for up to 1 week.

Seasonal Greens with Asian Pears, Toasted Pecans & Buttermilk Dressing

MAKES 4 TO 6 SERVINGS

Sometimes called pear apples, Asian pears are extremely refreshing, with a taste like a pear and the juiciness and texture of an apple. Unlike traditional pears, their crisp texture does not change after ripening. There are many varieties, ranging from the smaller brown russeted varieties to the larger clear-skinned yellow types, which I prefer for this salad.

1 large Asian pear, or any apple or pear

1/2 cup (2 ounces) coarsely chopped pecans, lightly toasted (see page 30), or substitute walnuts

8 cups seasonal greens, washed, torn, and spun dry

Buttermilk Dressing (recipe follows)

1/4 cup thinly sliced red onion, rinsed in cold water, then drained well

Quarter and core the Asian pear, then cut each quarter into 1/4-inch-thick slices. Toss the fruit with the pecans, greens, and 6 to 12 tablespoons of the dressing—depending on how heavily dressed you like your salad.

Divide the salad among chilled plates and top each serving with a little onion. Pass any remaining dressing on the side.

Buttermilk Dressing

MAKES 3/4 CUP

2 tablespoons cider vinegar

2 tablespoons Dijon mustard

2 tablespoons honey

1/4 cup vegetable oil

2 tablespoons buttermilk

1/4 teaspoon salt

In a small bowl, whisk the vinegar, mustard, and honey. Slowly drizzle in the oil while whisking constantly. After all the oil has been incorporated, whisk in the buttermilk and salt.

In the 1800s, pioneers brought pear trees west, and they soon thrived in the beneficent agricultural conditions of Washington, British Columbia, and Oregon: fertile soils, cool air, and warm sun. Today, commercial, organic, and multigenerational family orchards supply the juicy fruit to the Northwest's fresh pear industry. The varieties derive from those first cultivated in France and Belgium and are similarly cherished for their exquisite flavor, buttery texture, and long storage life.

The most familiar pears are the greenish-yellow-skinned Bartletts, but more and more selection is being seen in the markets. From brilliant Red Crimson and Red Bartlett to brownish-gold Bosc, from large Anjou to tiny Seckel, they range in both color and size.

Pears are one of the few fruits that do not mature well if ripened on the tree. Therefore, they are picked before they are ripe, then packed carefully, stored, and shipped, usually still unripened. That's why you'll often find firm, unripened pears in the store. It's easy to ripen them; place the pears in a paper bag and leave out at room temperature. Check daily, and when a pear yields to gentle pressure near the base of the stem, it is ready to eat. Refrigerate it until needed, and for best flavor, bring back to room temperature before eating. In general, summer pears such as Bartletts change color as they ripen, whereas winter pears do not. Therefore, depend on the gentle thumb test, not color, as your guide to ripeness.

Baby Arugula, Orange & Fennel Salad with Grilled Shrimp and White Balsamic Vinaigrette

MAKES 6 TO 8 SERVINGS

Arugula naturalizes easily in Northwest gardens and has "escaped" to grow wild in some parts of the region. It's even considered by some to be a weed! The green's rich, nutty flavor is complemented by a dressing of flavorful olive oil and sweet balsamic vinegar. I have used a white balsamic to keep the pretty colors of the shrimp and oranges.

Shrimp

1 tablespoon undiluted orange juice concentrate

Pinch of red pepper flakes

2 tablespoons minced orange zest

1 tablespoon Dijon mustard

2 tablespoons minced shallots

½ cup olive oil

2 tablespoons minced fennel fronds

1 tablespoon fennel seed, toasted and crushed (see page 30)

2½ teaspoons kosher salt

½ teaspoon black pepper

2 pounds large raw shrimp (32 to 40)

Salad

1 large or 2 small fennel bulbs, trimmed

6 oranges or tangerines

6 cups baby arugula

2 heads baby frisée, torn, rinsed, and spun dry

White Balsamic Vinaigrette (page 88)

To marinate the shrimp, whisk all the ingredients, except the shrimp, in a large bowl. Peel, devein, and remove tails, then add the shrimp to the marinade and toss to coat. Refrigerate and marinate for at least 1 hour or overnight.

To prepare the salad, finely shave the fennel bulbs with a sharp knife or a mandoline and crisp in ice water for 10 minutes. Spin dry before using. Cut the peel off the oranges, trim away all the white pith, then cut the fruit into ¼-inch-thick slices. Flick out any seeds. (If prepared ahead, refrigerate the fennel and orange slices separately, for up to 2 hours.)

Prepare a hot fire in a charcoal grill, or preheat a gas grill to high. Grill the shrimp until just pink and done, about 1 to 2 minutes per side.

Meanwhile, toss the arugula, frisée, fennel, and oranges with enough of the vinaigrette to coat nicely—taste for flavor, adding more dressing if needed.

Serve the salad on a large platter or divide among individual plates, arrange the shrimp on top, and drizzle with a little extra dressing, if desired.

Continued›

White Balsamic Vinaigrette

MAKES 2 CUPS

½ cup white balsamic vinegar

2 tablespoons minced shallots

1½ teaspoons Dijon mustard

¼ cup undiluted orange juice concentrate

Pinch of red pepper flakes, or 1 tablespoon
    harissa paste

2 teaspoons kosher salt

Freshly ground black pepper

1 tablespoon fennel seed, toasted and
    ground (see page 30)

1 cup extra-virgin olive oil

1 tablespoon chopped fennel fronds

In a large bowl, whisk the vinegar, shallots, mustard, and juice concentrate. Whisk in the pepper flakes, salt, pepper to taste, and fennel seed. Slowly drizzle in the oil, whisking constantly to emulsify. Stir in the fennel fronds. If made ahead, refrigerate until shortly before needed, then rewhisk before using.

CHEF'S NOTE: The vinaigrette keeps, refrigerated, for up to 2 weeks.

SIDE-STREET FENNEL

As I write this I am looking out my office window at the billowing plumes of fennel flowering along the sidewalk; the big stalks wildly poke their way up through a sliver of space in the concrete, making for quite a nice side street "garnish," to my mind. Feral fennel grows all over the Northwest, and although this plant is not the bulbing Florence fennel, its feathery fronds, pollen, and seeds are harvested for the kitchen.

Emerald City **Orzo Spinach Salad**

MAKES 8 TO 12 SERVINGS
Big flavors are especially good to meld into pasta salads. With exotic pistachios and sweet-tart apricots, this one would be a fine partner for grilled lamb, chicken, or salmon.

⅓ cup red wine vinegar

1 tablespoon Dijon mustard

2 tablespoons sugar

2 teaspoons kosher salt

1½ teaspoons curry powder

1 teaspoon hot sauce

2 teaspoons minced fresh garlic

⅓ cup sour cream or yogurt

3 tablespoons vegetable oil

½ teaspoon black pepper

1 pound (about 2 cups) dried orzo pasta

1 bunch spinach, stemmed, washed well, spun dry, and cut into ½-inch pieces

2 tablespoons coarsely chopped fresh cilantro

1 large yellow bell pepper, cut into small dice

1 large red bell pepper, cut into small dice

½ cup tiny-diced red onion

¾ cup pistachios, coarsely chopped

¾ cup finely-diced dried apricots

In a large bowl, whisk together the vinegar, mustard, sugar, salt, curry powder, hot sauce, garlic, sour cream, oil, and black pepper. Set aside.

Meanwhile, in a large pot of salted boiling water, cook the orzo according to package directions, or until just al dente. Drain but do not rinse. While the pasta is still fairly warm, toss it with the dressing. Let the mixture cool completely, then toss in the remaining ingredients.

Serve immediately, or refrigerate for up to 24 hours.

CHEF'S NOTE: This salad is at its best when tossed together an hour or two in advance and is still tasty up to twenty-four hours later, but I wouldn't make it further ahead than that. The secrets to delicious pasta salads are using bold flavors, cooking the pasta correctly, and combining the ingredients just long enough to let the flavors marry. If the components are mixed too soon, the salt in the dressing can leach moisture from the vegetables and the salad can become bland and watery. Or, even more often in my experience, the pasta absorbs most of the dressing and a dry, flavorless salad results.

Zingy Cucumber Salad

MAKES 2 TO 4 SERVINGS

At Dish D'Lish, my Food T' Go Go gourmet retail concept, this salad is a top seller. Its crisp sweet-and-tangy flavor is the quintessential accompaniment to sticky rice and the ever-popular neighborhood teriyaki chicken.

2 large cucumbers

$\frac{1}{2}$ cup unseasoned rice vinegar

$\frac{1}{3}$ cup sugar

$\frac{1}{3}$ cup very, very thinly sliced red onion

$\frac{1}{4}$ cup tiny-diced red bell pepper

$\frac{3}{4}$ teaspoon kosher salt

$\frac{1}{4}$ teaspoon red pepper flakes

With a vegetable peeler, strip off half of the cucumber peel, making lengthwise stripes. Halve the cucumbers lengthwise. Scoop out the seeds. Cut the cucumbers into $\frac{1}{3}$ - to $\frac{1}{2}$ -inch half-moons; you should have about 4 cups. Toss the cucumbers with the remaining ingredients and marinate, refrigerated, for 30 minutes.

Using a slotted spoon, serve the cucumbers from a large bowl or on individual plates as a side.

CHEF'S NOTE: You can make this up to 2 days before serving.

Seattle's Belltown P-Patch

Pacific Rim Chicken Salad with Crunchy Veggies, Napa Cabbage, and Low-Fat Sweet & Sour Sesame Dressing

MAKES 4 TO 6 SERVINGS

Chicken salads with a Pacific Rim or Asian imprint abound on Northwest lunch menus. There are as many versions as there are restaurants serving them. The common factors are usually thinly sliced napa cabbage included in the greens and some sort of sweet-and-sour, tangy dressing. Variations can include a topping of crunchy noodles, fried wonton strips, or roasted peanuts.

4 cups thinly sliced romaine lettuce

3 cups thinly sliced napa cabbage

½ cup very thinly sliced red cabbage

½ cup finely julienned carrot

½ cup very thinly sliced celery

1 cup peeled and seeded cucumber
    half-moons

1 can (8 ounces) sliced water chestnuts,
    drained well

3 cups thinly sliced cooked chicken breast

Low-Fat Sweet & Sour Sesame Dressing
    (recipe follows)

Garnishes

Green onions, cut into thin diagonal slices

Mixed black and toasted white sesame seeds

In a large bowl, toss the romaine, cabbages, carrot, celery, cucumber, water chestnuts, and chicken. Drizzle with the dressing and toss again. Divide among serving plates and garnish with green onions and sesame seeds.

Low-Fat Sweet & Sour Sesame Dressing

MAKES ¾ CUP

½ cup sugar

¾ teaspoon kosher salt

⅜ teaspoon coarsely ground black pepper

½ cup white wine vinegar

1 tablespoon canola oil

1½ teaspoons Asian sesame oil

1 tablespoon sesame seeds, toasted
    (see page 30)

In a small bowl, whisk the ingredients well. Keeps, refrigerated, for up to 2 weeks.

Endive Salad with Roasted Pears, Hazelnuts, Blue Cheese & Dish D'Lish Cranberry Vinaigrette

MAKES 4 TO 6 SERVINGS

Especially when sprinkled with Rogue River blue cheese, this characteristically local salad pops with the flavors of Oregon. In 2003, at the World Cheese Awards in London, the Rogue Creamery cheese was named the overall best blue cheese, making history when it beat out entries from all over Europe.

Pears

2 unpeeled ripe but firm pears

1 tablespoon olive oil

1 tablespoon balsamic vinegar

¼ teaspoon kosher salt

1 head baby frisée

2 heads Belgian endive

1 small head radicchio, sliced (about 2 cups)

4 cups baby arugula

Dish D'Lish Cranberry Vinaigrette (page 94)

½ cup crumbled blue cheese

⅓ cup dried cranberries

½ cup hazelnuts, toasted, skinned (see page 30), and coarsely chopped

To roast the pears, preheat an oven to 500°F. Cut the pears into eighths lengthwise. Core, then cut crosswise into 1-inch pieces. Whisk the remaining ingredients in a large bowl, then gently toss the pears in the mixture. Spread the pears on a rimmed baking sheet lightly sprayed with vegetable-oil cooking spray and roast for 7 to 10 minutes, or until lightly caramelized.

You can make the pears up to 1 day in advance. If you do, cool them thoroughly before refrigerating, then bring to room temperature about 1 hour before serving.

To finish the salad, cut the root end and about 1 inch of the top off the frisée. Rinse the frisée thoroughly, separate the head into leaves, and spin dry. Cut the stem ends off the endive, halve the heads lengthwise, then cut lengthwise into thin strips.

Toss the frisée and endive in a large, deep bowl with the remaining greens and about ½ cup of the vinaigrette.

Divide the greens among large dinner plates. Top each salad with pears, cheese, cranberries, and hazelnuts, dividing evenly. Pass additional dressing.

Continued›

CHEF'S NOTE: If you are having a big dinner party during the holidays, the entire recipe can easily be doubled. And, if you are tight on time, you can substitute sliced fresh pears or apples for the roasted pears.

Dish D'Lish Cranberry Vinaigrette

MAKES 1½ CUPS

⅔ cup fresh or frozen cranberries

¼ cup sugar

½ cup white wine vinegar or distilled white vinegar

1 teaspoon Dijon mustard

¼ cup orange juice

¾ cup vegetable oil or very light olive oil

¼ teaspoon salt

¼ teaspoon black pepper

Combine the cranberries, sugar, and vinegar in a small nonreactive saucepan and cook over medium heat until the cranberries pop, about 4 to 5 minutes. Remove from the heat and let cool.

Purée the mixture in a blender, then blend in the mustard and orange juice. With the machine running, gradually drizzle in the oil. The dressing should become smooth and emulsified. Blend in the salt and pepper. Refrigerate until needed.

Ravishing Radish Shaved-Veggie Salad with Lemon & Olive Oil

MAKES 6 SERVINGS

To make this salad in true "shaved" style, you will need a Japanese mandoline and a metal mesh glove (see page 33). Otherwise, take your time and slice the vegetables paper-thin with a very sharp small knife. Easter egg radishes available in the spring come in colors ranging from white to pink to deep purple and make for a beautiful variation.

1 bunch radishes, trimmed

1 fennel bulb, trimmed

1 pound large, firm button mushrooms

2 large heads Belgian endive

2 teaspoons very finely minced lemon zest

3 tablespoons fresh lemon juice

¼ cup extra-virgin olive oil

½ teaspoon kosher salt

2 tablespoons thinly sliced fresh chives

Freshly ground black pepper

Parmigiano-Reggiano or other grating cheese

CHEF'S NOTE: For a refreshing variation, you can also toss in a sprinkle of finely chopped fresh mint.

With a Japanese mandoline or a very sharp knife, cut the radishes and fennel into paper-thin slices. Submerge the slices in ice water for at least 30 minutes or up to 4 hours.

Meanwhile, cut the mushrooms into paper-thin slices. With a sharp knife, cut the Belgian endive into ⅛-inch-thick slices, being sure not to get the core. Refrigerate the endive and mushrooms separately until ready to serve.

When ready to serve, whisk the lemon zest and juice, oil, and salt in a large bowl. Drain the radishes and fennel, then spin dry in a salad spinner. Toss the shaved and sliced ingredients in the dressing. Sprinkle with the chives, season with pepper to taste, and toss to combine. Taste and adjust the seasoning and tartness with a touch more salt, pepper, and/or lemon juice if needed. Divide the salad among 6 chilled plates and shave some of the cheese over each salad. (Grate the cheese very finely with a Microplane grater, or use a potato peeler to make long, thin shavings.) Serve immediately.

Green Goddess Grilled Salmon Salad

MAKES 4 ENTRÉE SALAD SERVINGS
The creamy avocado and fresh tarragon in this retro dressing provide agreeable color and flavor contrasts to the salmon. I am repeatedly asked how to tell when your salmon is "done." Most of us Northwesterners like our salmon done on the less-cooked side, still slightly translucent in the center. Salmon fillets and steaks of different sizes (and shapes) will cook differently; just use good judgment and, if unsure, take a peek inside the center.

6 cups cut romaine lettuce or other favorite
    salad greens, rinsed and spun dry

½ cup finely shredded red cabbage

¼ cup coarsely grated or julienned carrot

12 cucumber slices

12 tomato wedges

12 black ripe olives

4 skinless wild salmon fillet portions
    (about 4 ounces each)

Salt

Freshly ground black pepper

Green Goddess Dressing (recipe follows)

Garnishes

4 lemon wedges

Fresh tarragon sprigs

Prepare a hot fire in a charcoal grill, or preheat a gas grill to high.

In a large bowl, toss the lettuce with the red cabbage and carrot. Divide the greens among 4 chilled dinner plates. Arrange the cucumber, tomato, and olives around the lettuce.

Brush the grill rack with a little oil. Season the salmon pieces with salt and pepper as desired, and place them "top-side down" on the hot grill. Cook the salmon, marking nicely on each side, until just done. Place a salmon fillet on each salad and dollop with the dressing. Garnish each plate with a lemon wedge and a sprig of tarragon. Pass the extra dressing.

Green Goddess Dressing

MAKES ABOUT 1½ CUPS

1 ripe avocado, peeled and pitted

3 tablespoons fresh lemon juice

2 tablespoons minced fresh tarragon

2 tablespoons minced fresh parsley

2 tablespoons minced fresh chives

1 teaspoon minced fresh garlic

2 anchovy fillets, finely minced,
    or 2 teaspoons anchovy paste

¼ teaspoon black pepper

½ cup mayonnaise

¼ cup sour cream

In a blender or food processor, combine all the ingredients except the mayonnaise and sour cream. Blend until the herbs are puréed and the mixture is smooth. Transfer to a bowl and whisk in the mayonnaise and sour cream until smooth. Refrigerate until needed, up to 2 days in advance.

Best-of-the-Season Tomato Salad with Roasted Corn & Peppers and Giant Toasted Chèvre Croutons

MAKES 6 SERVINGS

Whether eaten alone or served with a grilled steak, this is one of my favorite late-summer salads combining the season's bounty. If available, use fun-colored, yummy heirloom tomatoes, such as the red-and-yellow-striped Tigerella, nicknamed Mr. Stripey, or the Green Zebra, yellow Persimmon, or burgundy-red Brandywine.

1 green bell pepper

1 red bell pepper

1 yellow bell pepper

2 ears corn, husked

2 teaspoons Dijon mustard

1 clove fresh garlic, minced

3 tablespoons balsamic vinegar

2 teaspoons fresh lemon juice

1/3 cup extra-virgin olive oil

3/4 teaspoon salt

Freshly ground black pepper

1/4 cup chopped fresh basil

3 large vine-ripened heirloom tomatoes
   of various colors, cut into thick slices

Garnishes

Small fresh basil leaves or sprigs

Giant Toasted Chèvre Croutons (recipe
   follows) for serving

Prepare a hot fire in a charcoal grill, or preheat a gas grill to high. Roast the peppers on the grill, turning often until skin is totally blistered (see page 30). Peel, seed, and thinly slice peppers. Grill the corn, turning when each side is marked and lightly roasted. Cut the corn from the cob.

In a large bowl, whisk the mustard, garlic, vinegar, and lemon juice. Gradually whisk in the oil. Whisk in the salt and pepper to taste, then toss in the basil, roasted peppers, and corn.

Arranging the slices nicely, divide the tomatoes among 6 plates. Then divide the corn mixture among the salads, drizzling the tomatoes well with the dressing. Garnish with basil and serve the chèvre croutons alongside.

Giant Toasted Chèvre Croutons

Six 1/4-inch-thick, long diagonal slices
   baguette

1/2 cup (4 ounces) fresh goat cheese (chèvre)

Preheat an oven to 475°F. Spread the baguette slices with cheese, dividing it evenly. Place on a baking sheet and toast in the oven for about 6 minutes, or until the bread is crispy. Keep warm.

CHEF'S NOTE: To take this salad on a picnic or cookout or for a less formal presentation, cut the tomatoes in wedges and toss them gently with the corn mixture—and feel free to add a couple good handfuls of arugula. Toast the baguette slices on the grill before spreading with the cheese.

FISH
AND SHELLFISH

Calypso **Oyster Stew**

MAKES 6 CUPS, OR 4 ENTRÉE SERVINGS

In the Northwest, oyster stew is a Christmas Eve supper tradition. Still rich, but lighter than the traditional stew made with heavy cream, this version has lots of goodies.

One 16-ounce jar or 2 cups freshly shucked
    extra-small oysters with their liquor
½ to ¾ cup clam juice or chicken stock
2 slices raw bacon, minced (about ¼ cup)
½ cup diced white onion
1 cup domestic or wild mushrooms such as
    button mushrooms or chanterelles, thinly
    sliced (about 5 ounces)
½ cup thinly sliced celery
½ cup ¼-inch-diced carrot
½ cup ¼-inch-diced red bell pepper
¼ cup dry sherry
½ teaspoon dried thyme
¼ to ½ teaspoon Tabasco sauce
1 cup cooked large-diced or quartered
    red potatoes
1 tablespoon cornstarch
1¼ cups half-and-half
¾ teaspoon salt
¼ teaspoon black pepper

Garnishes
Chopped parsley
Lemon wedges

Drain the oysters, reserving the liquor. Set the oysters aside. Measure the liquor and add clam juice to make ¾ cup total. Set aside.

In a large, heavy saucepan or Dutch oven over medium-high heat, sauté the bacon for about 3 minutes, or until half cooked. Add the onion, mushrooms, celery, carrot, and bell pepper. Reduce the heat to medium and sauté the vegetable mixture for about 4 minutes, stirring often. Stir in the sherry and thyme, then add the reserved oyster liquor, the Tabasco, and potatoes. Increase the heat to high and bring to a low boil.

Whisk the cornstarch into the half-and-half in a bowl, then whisk the mixture into the gently boiling stew. Immediately add the oysters and heat just until the oysters plump and their edges are ruffled. Season with the salt and pepper, adjusting for taste.

Spoon into serving bowls and sprinkle with the chopped parsley. Serve with lemon wedges for squeezing.

Spot Prawn Pasta with Lemon Cream

MAKES 4 SERVINGS

Spot prawns, so called because of the distinctive white spots on their pink shells, are the largest shrimp in Puget Sound and might reach a length of more than nine inches, excluding the antennae. Although their season is usually just a short period in late spring, this is one of the most important shrimp species for both sport and commercial fishermen. And luckily, the spot prawn season comes right in line with the local asparagus and wild morel mushrooms featured in this pasta.

12 ounces dried linguine pasta

Splash of olive oil, plus 2 tablespoons

Salt

1 cup thinly sliced fresh morel mushrooms or substitute cremini or button mushrooms (about 4 to 5 ounces)

1 tablespoon minced fresh garlic

1/8 teaspoon red pepper flakes

1/4 cup clam juice

1/4 cup fresh lemon juice

1/4 cup dry white wine

1 cup heavy whipping cream

1 cup thinly diagonally sliced asparagus

1/2 cup shelled fresh peas or frozen peas, thawed and drained

1/2 cup julienned red bell pepper

1 pound spot prawns or other large shrimp, peeled and deveined

1 tablespoon minced lemon zest

3 tablespoons thinly sliced fresh chives

Freshly ground black pepper

In a large pot of salted boiling water, cook the pasta according to package directions, or until just al dente. Drain well, toss very lightly with a splash of olive oil and salt to taste, then cover and keep warm.

Meanwhile, start the sauce. Heat the 2 tablespoons olive oil in a large, nonstick skillet or sauté pan over high heat. Sauté the mushrooms until lightly browned, about 2 minutes. Add the garlic and pepper flakes and sauté 30 seconds more.

Add the clam juice, lemon juice, and wine and cook to reduce to one-fourth of the original volume, about 2 minutes. Whisk in the cream, then add the asparagus, fresh peas if using, bell pepper, prawns, and lemon zest and cook for 2 minutes.

Add the cooked pasta and cook for about 1 1/2 minutes more, until the sauce is coating the pasta and the liquid is almost all absorbed. Toss in 2 tablespoons of the chives and the thawed frozen peas if using. Season to taste with salt and pepper.

Serve the pasta on warm plates, being sure to get some "goodies" on each portion. Sprinkle with the remaining chives.

CHEF'S NOTE: You can roast the shrimp shells in a preheated 375°F oven on a baking sheet for about 20 to 30 minutes, then mix them in a saucepan with the cream and bring to a simmer. Turn off the heat and let the shells infuse the cream with flavor for 30 minutes, then strain and use the cream for the pasta sauce. (Discard the shrimp shells.) This dish is equally good made with 8 ounces of smoked salmon in place of the shrimp—just be sure to watch the salt level.

Pale Ale Oven-Roasted Clams

MAKES 4 SERVINGS AS A SHARED APPETIZER, OR 2 AS A LIGHT ENTRÉE

With more than two hundred small craft breweries in the region, beer ends up in a lot of our dishes. India pale ale adds a slight bitterness that makes for a pleasantly hoppy broth—unequaled for sopping up with lots of crusty bread. I like to serve the clams directly from the skillet in the center of the table for sharing.

2 pounds small Manila clams, rinsed

1 tablespoon minced fresh garlic

$1/8$ to $1/4$ teaspoon red pepper flakes,
   or to taste

2 ripe plum tomatoes, chopped (about 1 cup)

1 teaspoon minced fresh rosemary

$1/2$ lemon, cut into 4 pieces

$1/4$ cup flavorful pale ale, such as Bridgeport
   India Pale Ale

2 tablespoons butter, cut into small chunks,
   or olive oil

1 large rosemary sprig (optional)

Preheat an oven to 500°F. Toss the clams, garlic, pepper flakes, tomatoes, and minced rosemary in a large bowl. Transfer to a large cast-iron or other heavy skillet with an ovenproof handle. Squeeze the lemon pieces over the clams, then drop the pieces into the pan. Pour the beer over the clams and scatter with the butter. Place the rosemary sprig (if using) in the center.

Roast for 14 to 16 minutes, or until the clams are all open. Remove from the oven, and stir gently with a large spoon. Discard any clams that do not open. Serve in the skillet, set on a hot pad or trivet—being sure to wrap the skillet handle with a cloth napkin or pot holder.

Citrus Teriyaki Salmon with Pineapple Salsa

MAKES 6 SERVINGS

The Northwest is teriyaki-crazy! They say there's espresso sold on every corner, but teriyaki's right there with it. Typically, teriyaki sauce is made in a very sweet style; my version is less so and more on the citrusy side. The flavors of teriyaki—sweet, salty, and tangy—interplay with the rich flavor of salmon.

Marinade

2 tablespoons dry sherry wine or sake

¼ cup honey

2 tablespoons packed brown sugar

4 teaspoons minced peeled fresh ginger

2 teaspoons minced fresh garlic

¼ teaspoon red pepper flakes

1½ teaspoons Asian sesame oil

2 tablespoons orange juice

2 tablespoons fresh lemon juice

½ cup soy sauce

6 portions wild salmon fillets or steaks
    (6 to 8 ounces each)

Canola oil for cooking

Pineapple Salsa (facing page)

Garnishes

Lime wedges

Fresh cilantro sprigs

To make the marinade, in a microwave-safe container, stir the sherry, honey, brown sugar, ginger, garlic, pepper flakes, and sesame oil. Cover and microwave on high for about 30 seconds to 1 minute, or until the brown sugar is dissolved and mixture is hot. Whisk in the remaining marinade ingredients and let cool to room temperature.

Put the fish in a glass baking dish or a large resealable plastic bag and add the cooled marinade. Turn the fish pieces in the marinade to coat all sides. Refrigerate for at least 1½ hours or up to 4 hours. (Note: If the salmon is thick, it can marinate for up to 8 hours.)

Preheat an oven to 450°F. Heat a large, heavy ovenproof nonstick skillet over medium-high heat. Add a little oil. Remove the fish from the marinade, draining off excess. Discard the marinade.

Sear the salmon pieces for about 1½ minutes per side, or until nicely browned. (Be careful not to overbrown—you just want to get some nice color on the pieces, not to totally cook them.)

Transfer the skillet to the oven and cook salmon until just done, about 3 to 8 minutes, depending on the thickness of the fish and degree of doneness desired.

Transfer the fish to individual plates and top each serving with about ¼ cup pineapple salsa. Garnish with lime wedges and cilantro sprigs.

Pineapple Salsa

2 tablespoons finely diced red bell pepper

1 cup ¼-inch-diced fresh pineapple

½ teaspoon finely grated orange zest

1 orange, peeled and cut into ¼-inch dice

2 tablespoons fresh lime juice

1 teaspoon cider vinegar

1 tablespoon finely diced red onion

½ teaspoon minced peeled fresh ginger

2 tablespoons chopped fresh cilantro

¼ teaspoon red pepper flakes, or ½ to 1 teaspoon minced fresh jalapeño chile

2 teaspoons packed brown sugar

1 teaspoon granulated sugar

¼ teaspoon salt

In a medium glass bowl, mix the ingredients well. Serve immediately, or refrigerate for up to 2 hours.

Hazelnut-Crusted Halibut with Apple Vinaigrette

MAKES 4 SERVINGS

Fished for in Alaska and British Columbia, halibut are the largest of all flatfish. The biggest ever recorded for the northern Pacific was a 495-pound fish caught near Petersburg, Alaska. Halibut has a mild, fresh flavor and is the second favorite fish in the Northwest, surpassed only by salmon.

Vinaigrette

1 unpeeled red apple, halved and cored
3 tablespoons hazelnut oil
2 teaspoons minced shallot
2 teaspoons sugar
1/4 cup fresh lemon juice
2 teaspoons Dijon mustard
1/2 cup olive oil
1 1/2 teaspoons minced fresh lemon thyme
    or regular thyme
1/4 teaspoon salt
Pinch of cayenne pepper
1 tablespoon water

Crust

1 1/2 cups (8 ounces) hazelnuts, lightly
    toasted and skinned (see page 30)
Pinch of dry mustard
1 1/4 teaspoons salt
1/4 teaspoon cayenne pepper
1 tablespoon grated lemon zest
1 teaspoon dried thyme leaves

4 skinless 1/2-inch-thick halibut fillet portions
    (4 to 6 ounces each)
4 tablespoons (1/2 stick) butter, melted
Fresh lemon thyme or regular thyme sprigs
    for garnishing

To make the vinaigrette, chop half of the apple; reserve the other half. In a small skillet, heat the hazelnut oil over medium-low heat and add the chopped apple. Cook for 1 minute, then add the shallot and sugar. Continue cooking until the apple is soft, about 1 minute. Add the lemon juice and remove from the heat.

Let cool, then purée in a blender until smooth. Pour the puréed mixture into a medium bowl, add the mustard, then slowly whisk in the olive oil. Add the thyme and season with the salt and cayenne. If the vinaigrette is too thick, thin it slightly with water. Cut the remaining apple half into 1/4-inch dice. Toss into the dressing. Refrigerate until needed.

To make the crust, combine the crust ingredients in a food processor and pulse until finely chopped but not so fine as a meal. Set aside in a large shallow dish.

Preheat an oven to 425°F. Grease a rimmed baking sheet with oil. Dip each piece of fish in the melted butter, coating well. Immediately press each piece firmly into the crust mixture, turning to coat all sides well. Place the coated halibut pieces on the baking sheet and bake for about 6 minutes, or until the fish is just cooked through. Carefully transfer the fish to individual plates and drizzle some of the vinaigrette over them. Garnish with thyme sprigs. Pass the extra vinaigrette.

Geoduck Steak Piccata

MAKES 4 SERVINGS

Zowie! It's not really a duck—but a giant clam! And what a wild-looking mollusk it is. This recipe uses the belly part of the geoduck, which makes a very tender steak. If you aren't up to digging a couple of these big boys, then large calamari steaks are a good substitute.

¼ cup milk

2 eggs, lightly beaten

½ cup flour

1½ teaspoons salt

¼ teaspoon black pepper

4 geoduck steaks, about 4 ounces each, lightly pounded ¼ to ⅓ inch thick

4 tablespoons (½ stick) butter

2 tablespoons olive oil

2 teaspoons minced fresh garlic

⅓ cup fresh lemon juice

⅓ cup dry white wine

2 tablespoons capers, drained

¼ cup coarsely chopped fresh flat-leaf parsley

In a small, shallow bowl, whisk the milk and eggs. In another shallow bowl, mix the flour, salt, and pepper.

Dip the geoduck pieces into the milk mixture and then into the flour mixture. Coat each piece well, then shake off the excess.

Meanwhile, in a large, shallow nonstick sauté pan or skillet, melt 2 tablespoons of the butter with the olive oil over medium-high heat. Add the coated geoduck pieces to the hot skillet, and cook quickly for about 1 to 1½ minutes on each side, depending on the size of the steaks, until golden, just cooked through, and still very tender. Drain the geoduck on paper towels. Keep warm.

Reduce the heat to medium-low, stir in the garlic, and cook for about 1 minute until sweated but not browned. Add the lemon juice and wine and cook to reduce to half. Remove from heat and whisk in the remaining 2 tablespoons butter. Swirl in the capers and parsley.

Serve the geoduck on a platter or individual plates and spoon some sauce over each portion. Serve immediately.

Coriander, Curry & Yogurt-Crusted Snapper with Fresh Mint

MAKES 4 SERVINGS

Vancouver, British Columbia, has some of the best East Indian food you'll find anywhere. The dazzling Indian-fusion dishes served at Vij's Restaurant were my inspiration for this recipe.

¾ cup plain yogurt

1 teaspoon minced fresh garlic

½ teaspoon ground cumin

1 tablespoon coriander seed, crushed

2 teaspoons mild curry powder

1½ teaspoons salt

½ teaspoon black pepper

1 to 2 tablespoons olive oil

4 Pacific rockfish "snapper" fillets
   (about 6 ounces each)

Chopped fresh mint for garnishing

In a small bowl, stir the yogurt, garlic, and cumin. In another small bowl, combine the coriander seed, curry powder, salt, and pepper.

In a very large nonstick skillet or sauté pan, heat the oil over medium-high heat. Meanwhile, dip the fish into the yogurt mixture to lightly coat each side, then sprinkle each side with the curry mixture, dividing the seasoning evenly. (Use all the seasoning.)

Immediately place the fish in the hot pan and cook until opaque throughout, about 2½ minutes on each side. Serve with a light sprinkling of chopped mint.

CHEF'S NOTE: I like to serve this with a basmati rice pilaf and sautéed spinach.

MUSSELS

Plump, briny morsels of seafood goodness!

Succulent mussels are a Northwest menu staple—from casual brewpubs serving up bowlfuls simmered with loads of garlic and microbrew and accompanied with big chunks of artisanal bread for mopping up the juices to fine-dining restaurants featuring the bivalves as sexy appetizers, entrée embellishments, or black jewels glimmering from towering iced-shellfish extravaganzas. But it wasn't always so.

When I was growing up, mussels were considered too much trouble to harvest. Now, they're customarily "farmed" on ropes. Two types of this mollusk are grown in the Northwest: the locals, *Mytilus trossulus,* and the Mediterraneans, *M. galloprovincialis.* With the locals at their peak in winter and the Mediterraneans in summer, mussels are available year-round.

Mussels must be debearded (the fuzzy part that attaches them to rocks or ropes pulled off), rinsed, and scrubbed clean. Local mussels should be cooked only until their shells pop open and the meats are just plumped. If overcooked, they will be tough. Mediterraneans, however, are not yet done when the shells just open; they should be cooked until you see that the meat is contracting, plumped, and cooked through. Otherwise, the meats could be flaccid and not giving their full flavor. Cooked mussel meats range in color from pale cream to bright orange.

A big bowl of steamed shellfish makes a great starter for a group participatory meal that's entertaining to eat. When eating mussels, it's fun to use an empty, hinged shell as a natural utensil to pick the mussel meat up and pop it into your mouth. But if you have major shellfish-lovers there, you've got to be quick! Be sure to put out plenty of bowls for collecting the empty shells.

Steamed Mussels with Italian Sausage & Fettunta

MAKES 4 TO 6 SERVINGS

Sometimes when you eat mussels, you might think you are finding a large piece of grit, but whoa! it might be a tiny pearl or even a minuscule crab! A much-valued feature in cooking them is that they are fast, fast, fast. They should be cooked only until their shells pop open and the meat is just plumped. This recipe was inspired by my friend, chef Don Curtiss. Bold-flavored sausage, garlic, and tomatoes make for a rich broth.

1 can (14½ ounces) peeled Italian plum
    tomatoes
¼ cup olive oil
8 ounces Italian sausage, bulk or removed
    from casings
2 teaspoons minced fresh garlic
3 pounds mussels, scrubbed and debearded
    (see page 30)
¼ cup chopped fresh flat-leaf parsley
½ teaspoon red pepper flakes, or to taste
1 cup dry white wine
¼ teaspoon freshly ground black pepper
Fettunta (recipe follows)

In a blender or food processor, purée the tomatoes with their juice until coarsely puréed. Set aside.

In a very large skillet or Dutch oven with a tight-fitting lid, heat the olive oil over medium-high heat. Sauté the sausage, stirring and breaking it up, until browned and three-quarters cooked, about 3 to 4 minutes. Add the garlic, mussels, parsley, and pepper flakes and sauté for about 30 seconds more. Add the wine, reserved tomatoes, and pepper. Cover and cook until the mussels have opened, about 3 to 6 minutes. Discard any mussels that do not open.

Serve the mussels in large, shallow bowls. Pass a basket or platter of warm fettunta.

Fettunta

MAKES 4 TO 6 SERVINGS

This dish is so simple, yet the exact procedure of assembling it makes the flavors come together perfectly. I first sampled this in Tuscany at an olive oil factory where they grilled it in a huge fireplace in the "employee" lunchroom!

8 slices rustic Italian bread
2 to 3 cloves fresh garlic
Sea salt or kosher salt for sprinkling
Extra-virgin olive oil for drizzling

Prepare a hot fire in a charcoal grill. Add some wood chips or fruit-wood pieces to the coals to give some smoke. On the grill rack, grill the bread on each side until toasty. Rub each slice of the toasted bread with a garlic clove. (It can be fun for guests to do this.) Sprinkle lightly with salt and drizzle liberally with oil. Serve while still warm!

Grilled Salmon with Herbed Walla Walla Sweet Onions

MAKES 6 SERVINGS

When the weather is good, Northwesterners head out to their grills, and you can usually find them cooking salmon. The famous Copper River and Yukon River salmon runs just happen to coincide with the harvest of local sweet onions—a match made in heaven.

Onions

1 large Walla Walla Sweet onion, cut into
   ½ -inch-thick rings
¼ cup white wine vinegar
3 tablespoons sugar
½ teaspoon kosher salt
¼ teaspoon red pepper flakes
2 tablespoons olive oil
2 tablespoons coarsely chopped fresh basil
   or cilantro
1 tablespoon coarsely chopped fresh tarragon
1 tablespoon ½ -inch-long pieces fresh chives
2 tablespoons coarsely chopped fresh
   flat-leaf parsley

Salmon

2 tablespoons olive oil
6 skinless salmon fillet portions
   (about 4 to 6 ounces each)
Kosher salt
Freshly ground black pepper

Garnish

Lots of fresh herb sprigs

To make the onions, carefully separate the rings and place in a resealable plastic bag. In a small bowl, whisk the vinegar, sugar, salt, pepper flakes, and oil. Pour the marinade over the onion and close the bag, expelling excess air. Turn the bag to coat the onion evenly, then refrigerate for at least 30 minutes, or up to 4 hours, turning the bag occasionally. Just before grilling the salmon, gently toss the onion and marinade in a large bowl with the chopped herbs.

To grill the salmon, prepare a hot fire in a charcoal grill, or preheat a gas grill to high. Meanwhile, pour the olive oil onto a large plate. Swipe each side of the salmon fillets through the oil, then season well with salt and pepper. Grill the fish for about 1 to 4 minutes per side, or to the desired doneness, moving the fillets to create crisscross marks. Different-sized fillets will cook differently—just use good judgment and try not to overcook your salmon.

Place the grilled salmon on plates and divide the onion evenly among them, piling high and spooning marinade over all. Garnish with herb sprigs and serve immediately.

CHEF'S NOTE: For a summer buffet table, grill a whole side of salmon and serve it on a large platter, festooned with the herbed onions and fresh herb sprigs.

CLAMS

Clam digging has long been a leading Northwest pastime. And clam eating, of course, motivates the activity.

Native littlenecks and black-striped Manilas are the standard steamers. Some people prefer them steamed very simply, just the shellfish with a little splash of white wine and a good pinch of garlic. However, clams are versatile carriers of flavor, so they are also delicious in more exotic preparations. Northwest diners have been the beneficiaries of some of the wonderful things Asian cuisines do with shellfish, such as steaming clams with coconut milk, lemongrass, and Thai yellow curry.

The Pacific razor clam, *Siliqua patula,* lives all along the region's ocean beaches. It has a long, narrow shell that resembles a straight-edge razor. Adult clams live anywhere from right in the pounding surf to a few feet above the low-tide line.

These are common sport-digging clams that are dug at low tide when their "holes," the dimples left in the sand when the neck is retracted, are seen in the sand or shallow surf. With fragile, thin and brittle shells, they can be anywhere from a few inches to a few feet down, making for a challenging dig. The faster the clam descends in its burrow, the harder the clam digger has to work to extract this tasty bivalve.

Razor clams are also harvested commercially, and occasionally, when you're really lucky, you'll see them on menus—usually in beach-town cafes. Simply prepared, by being dipped in egg and bread crumbs and lightly sautéed in butter, then finished with a quick squeeze of lemon and chopped fresh parsley, they need nothing else!

The Northwest does have its share of curiously strange shellfish species. The geoduck clam is known to get up to nine pounds, with the preferred harvest weight being two pounds. Named after a Nisqually word meaning "dig deep," it lives up to an average of 40 years—with a record age of 135 years—at depths of four to six feet in the marine mud up and down the coast, with the largest populations in Puget Sound and the waters of British Columbia. These bivalves bring big-eyed stares and looks of awe from tourists at Fisherman's Wharf in Richmond, B.C.'s historic Steveston Village, or at Seattle's Pike Place Market, where the clams' hose-like necks hang over the sides of ice barrels.

Geoduck meat is often chopped for hearty chowders, but the Asian community probably deals with this giant clam the best, slicing it thinly and serving it pristinely as sashimi or quickly stir-frying it with salted black beans, scallions, and garlic. You can also cook it up as a steak, as in Geoduck Steak Piccata (page 108). At seaside diners, you can sometimes see menu specials touting geoduck burgers!

Clam chowders seem to stir up fervent debates among locals. Northwesterners can be quite set in their ways when it comes to chowder. Usually, it's white—at least we can agree on that; but as to the thickness, the type of clam (any of the above), and the seasoning (to dill or not to dill), the discussions can become passionately heated. Yet we always end up with a sumptuous bowl of steamy goodness.

Beachfront Seafood Stew

MAKES 4 TO 6 SERVINGS

Whether you make this stew for a dinner party or make the base ahead to take along to the beach to enjoy after a day of clamming and mussel-gathering, the dish calls out for a bottle of Northwest white wine, such as Columbia Crest semillon-chardonnay or, if you're a red wine drinker like me, a bottle of Cavatappi red.

Base

¼ cup olive oil

1 cup chopped white onion

½ cup chopped red bell pepper

1 tablespoon minced fresh garlic

1 cup thinly sliced mushrooms

1 small fennel bulb, thinly sliced

1½ teaspoons finely grated orange zest

½ cup dry white wine

2 cups clam juice

3 cups chopped ripe tomatoes or diced
    canned plum tomatoes with juice

Pinch of saffron threads (optional)

1 teaspoon salt

Dash of Tabasco sauce

½ teaspoon minced fresh rosemary

1 teaspoon minced fresh thyme

Fresh-cracked black pepper

1 tablespoon minced fresh basil

Seafood

¼ cup olive oil

12 ounces littleneck clams in the shell

8 ounces mussels, scrubbed and debearded
    (see page 30)

8 large shrimp, peeled and deveined

4 ounces sea scallops, halved

8 ounces boneless, skinless firm-fleshed fish,
    cut into 2-inch pieces

6 small cooked red potatoes, halved

¼ cup Pernod liqueur (optional)

Fresh rosemary sprigs for garnishing

To prepare the base, heat the oil in a large pot or Dutch oven over medium heat. Add the onion, bell pepper, garlic, mushrooms, fennel, and orange zest. Cook, stirring often, for 4 to 5 minutes, or until tender.

Add the wine, clam juice, tomatoes, saffron (if using), salt, Tabasco, rosemary, thyme, and pepper to taste. Turn the heat to high and bring the mixture to a low boil, then reduce the heat to low and simmer for 6 to 8 minutes. Remove from the heat, stir in the basil, and adjust the seasoning if necessary. If not using immediately, cool and refrigerate until needed. Reheat before proceeding.

To finish with the seafood, heat the oil in a large pot or Dutch oven over medium-high heat. Add the remaining ingredients, except for the potatoes and Pernod. Lightly sauté for 30 seconds, turning the fish and scallop pieces as necessary. Add the potatoes and Pernod (if using) and cook 30 seconds more, then add the hot stew base.

Cover the pot and cook until the clams and mussels just open. (Take care not to overcook the seafood.) Immediately remove from the heat. Discard any clams or mussels that have not opened. Divide the fish and shellfish among individual large bowls, then ladle in the broth and vegetables. Serve immediately, garnished with rosemary sprigs.

CHEF'S NOTE: Serve this with thick slices of crusty French bread for soaking up the juices.

Friday Night Oysters & Fried Green Tomatoes with
Ultimate Tartar Sauce

MAKES 4 SERVINGS

When I was growing up, this dish was a Friday-night staple in the early fall when green tomatoes flourish in Northwest gardens. The recipe also features fresh jarred oysters, which come in a variety of sizes; extra-smalls are used here. Tartar sauce is a locally coveted condiment, used more frequently on French fries than ketchup is; "connoisseurs" will tell you it must be homemade.

1 cup flour

1/2 cup yellow cornmeal

2 teaspoons salt

1/2 teaspoon coarsely ground black pepper

1/2 teaspoon paprika or smoked Spanish paprika (pimentón)

3 to 4 large green tomatoes, cut into 1/2-inch-thick crosswise slices (about 12 slices)

Vegetable oil or a mixture of oil and bacon drippings for frying

Two 10-ounce jars or 1 pint shucked extra-small oysters, drained

Ultimate Tartar Sauce (facing page)

Preheat an oven to 165° to 200°F. In a plate or shallow bowl, mix the flour, cornmeal, salt, pepper, and paprika with a fork.

Dredge the tomato slices, a few at a time, in the seasoned flour to coat well. Set the tomatoes aside on a lightly floured baking sheet. Reserve the flour mixture.

In a large skillet, heat 1/4 to 1/3 inch oil over medium heat. Fry the tomato slices for about 2 to 5 minutes, or until golden brown on each side, turning as necessary. As the tomatoes are done, transfer them to an ovenproof platter or baking sheet lined with paper towels and keep warm in the low oven.

When all the tomatoes are fried, discard the oil and wipe the pan clean, then heat 1/4 to 1/3 inch of fresh oil in the skillet over medium-high heat. Working in batches, dredge the oysters in the reserved seasoned flour, tossing them gently with a fork and shaking off any excess. When a batch of oysters is floured and the oil is hot, carefully fry the oysters, taking care not to crowd the pan, cooking until the oysters are lightly browned and the edges start to curl, about 1 to 1 1/2 minutes on each side.

Transfer them to the paper-towel-lined platter, spacing the oysters apart, and keep warm in the oven while you continue frying the remaining oysters. Be sure to let the oil reheat as necessary between batches of oysters. If you are confident about frying, you can use a second pan and fry the oysters at the same time as the tomatoes.

Divide the oysters and tomatoes among individual plates and serve immediately, accompanied with the tartar sauce.

Ultimate Tartar Sauce

MAKES 1 CUP

¾ cup mayonnaise

2 tablespoons finely chopped dill pickle or
    dill pickle relish

1 tablespoon drained capers, chopped

½ green onion, very thinly sliced

¾ teaspoon Dijon mustard

¼ teaspoon Tabasco sauce

1 tablespoon chopped parsley

⅛ teaspoon celery seed

1 tablespoon fresh lemon juice

¼ teaspoon granulated garlic

⅛ teaspoon salt

⅛ teaspoon black pepper

In a small bowl, mix all the ingredients. The sauce can be made up to 4 days in advance and refrigerated until needed.

CHEF'S NOTE: This tartar sauce is quite tangy; reduce the lemon juice if you prefer a milder version. Fresh Corn Salsa (page 161) would be delicious with the oysters and green tomatoes as well.

Almost-Naked Crab with a Collection of Sauces

There is nothing better than fresh crab, whether it is sweet Dungeness or meaty king crab legs. Fresh, right out of the shell is still my first-choice way to eat these prized Northwest creatures, but I really love crab any way I can get it! And if you're a crab-lover, you've probably noticed that some crab-eaters are pickers and some are pilers. The former pick and eat as they go, while the latter make a pile of shelled crab, not tasting even a single morsel until they have a good-sized mound. Now's the chance to see which your friends are!

Live or cooked Dungeness crabs and/or Alaskan king crab legs (plan for at least ¹/₂ large Dungeness crab or 3 large king crab legs per person)

Louis Dressing (page 83)

Butter, melted

Lemon Herb Splash (page 120)

Lemon wedges

Tools

Crab/lobster crackers, or nut crackers

Seafood forks and/or scoops

Picks

Lots of napkins

To cook live Dungeness crabs, bring enough water to cover the amount of crabs you are cooking to a boil in a very large pot. Immerse the crabs, cover the pot, and return the water to a full boil. Reduce the heat to a simmer and start timing. Cook for 10 to 20 minutes, depending on the size of your crabs.

Remove the crabs and immediately plunge them into a large pot or other container of ice water to quickly cool down.

To clean a Dungeness crab, remove the top shell and discard or wash it to use as a serving vessel. Remove and discard the gills (the gray fingery things). Break off the mouth part and the apron-flap on the underside. Scrape out the viscera (the goopy business). If need be, rinse in cool water.

Twist off the legs and claws, and then break the body in half. If not serving immediately, refrigerate, lightly covered with a clean damp towel, until ready to serve, for up to 2 days.

To serve king crab, split the legs lengthwise with a knife or kitchen shears. Serve chilled, or warm by lightly steaming the legs for a few minutes.

Serve the crab with the dipping sauces of your choice, lemon wedges, and any "tools" needed.

Continued›

Lemon Herb Splash

MAKES ½ CUP, ENOUGH FOR UP TO 8 CRAB-EATERS

6 tablespoons extra-virgin olive oil

2 teaspoons minced lemon zest

2 tablespoons fresh lemon juice

1½ teaspoons minced fresh rosemary

1½ teaspoons minced fresh basil

1 tablespoon minced fresh parsley

2 teaspoons minced lemon verbena (optional)

½ teaspoon minced fresh garlic

⅛ teaspoon red pepper flakes

¼ teaspoon salt

Mix all the ingredients well. Keep, refrigerated, for up to 2 days if made ahead. Bring to room temperature 30 minutes before serving.

UNDERWATER FORAGING

Northwest divers have had a treasure trove of sea jewels to pluck over the years. Though the harvesting of some wild bounty, such as abalone and Puget Sound king and box crabs, is closed now, there are still a lot of appetizing things to collect under the cold Pacific waters. The trophies run from rock scallops and swimming scallops to wiggly and weird but tasty sea cucumbers to spiny sea urchins prized for their roe. (Some say the latter is an aphrodisiac if enough is consumed.)

Seared Scallops with Chinese Black Bean Vinaigrette

MAKES 6 TO 8 FIRST-COURSE OR 4 ENTRÉE SERVINGS

The large weathervane scallops harvested in Alaska from Yakutat Bay to the eastern Aleutians are typically marketed "chemical-free," making for less "weeping" in the pan when searing and therefore better caramelization. The Chinese flavors of fermented black beans and orange zest add a roundness to this dish. Be sure to rinse the black beans very well to remove the super-saltiness before mincing them for the vinaigrette.

Vinaigrette

6 tablespoons canola oil

3/4 cup stemmed and chopped shiitake
    mushrooms (about 3 ounces)

1 1/2 tablespoons minced shallots

1 tablespoon minced peeled fresh ginger

1 tablespoon minced fresh garlic

1/2 cup 1/2-inch-sliced green onions

6 tablespoons dry sherry

1 1/2 tablespoons soy sauce

1 tablespoon sugar

3 tablespoons unseasoned rice vinegar

1 1/2 tablespoons salted black beans,
    rinsed well and minced

2 teaspoons minced orange zest

Asian hot chili paste

Scallops

2 pounds very large sea scallops, such
    as Alaska weathervanes (28 to 30)

1 tablespoon canola oil

Heaping 1/4 teaspoon kosher salt

To make the vinaigrette, in a large nonstick sauté pan, heat 3 tablespoons of the oil over medium-high heat. Sauté the mushrooms, stirring often, until tender, about 1 minute. Add the shallots, ginger, garlic, and green onions, and sauté for 1 to 1 1/2 minutes more, stirring often. Cook only until the vegetables are softened; do not brown the garlic.

Quickly add the sherry, soy sauce, sugar, and vinegar. Bring to a boil and cook for 1 to 2 minutes until slightly reduced. Turn off the heat and stir in the black beans. Transfer the mixture to a bowl and let cool. Whisk in the remaining 3 tablespoons oil and the orange zest. Season to taste with the chili paste.

To cook the scallops, heat a large nonstick skillet or sauté pan over high heat until very hot. Meanwhile, toss the scallops, oil, and salt in a large bowl to coat scallops evenly.

Cook the scallops in batches, or use two pans. Place the scallops in the hot pan, a few at a time; do not crowd. Cook until seared, about 2 minutes on the first side, then 1 1/2 to 2 minutes on the second side. Transfer the scallops to a plate and keep just warm while you cook the remaining scallops. Scallops of different sizes will cook differently—just use good judgment and try to not overcook them.

Divide the scallops among dinner plates. Whisk the vinaigrette well and drizzle evenly over and around the scallops.

CHEF'S NOTE: It is very important to cook the scallops in a very, very hot pan to get a nice sear on each side. When done, they should remain translucent in the center. I like to serve these with steamed jasmine rice and garlic-sautéed baby bok choy or Chinese broccoli.

Pan-Roasted Halibut with Morel Mushroom Cream

MAKES 4 SERVINGS

The morel, one of the richest-tasting wild mushrooms, is a spring delight after our long gray winters. Just a few morels will do you in a recipe, for their flavor is intense. They come into season about the second week in April, depending on the weather, and the season lasts about four to six weeks. Always cook fresh morels; raw morels sometimes cause an upset stomach. If desired, serve the halibut with additional sautéed fresh morels on the side.

Sauce

1 tablespoon butter

1 shallot, minced

1 clove fresh garlic, minced

½ cup chopped fresh morel mushrooms
    (about 3 ounces), or ¼ ounce dried morels,
    soaked in the white wine and then
    chopped

3 tablespoons brandy

½ cup dry white wine

2 cups heavy whipping cream

1 teaspoon fresh lemon juice

½ teaspoon salt

Pinch of white pepper

Fish

4 skinless halibut fillet portions
    (6 to 8 ounces each)

Salt

Freshly ground black pepper

1 tablespoon olive oil

Garnish

Fresh chives

To make the sauce, melt the butter in a heavy saucepan over medium heat. Sauté the shallot, garlic, and mushrooms, stirring often, for 1 to 2 minutes, or until the shallot is translucent. Add the brandy and wine and cook to reduce for about 5 minutes. Add the cream and bring to a simmer, then reduce the heat and slowly simmer, stirring often, for 20 to 30 minutes, or until the sauce is reduced to about 1½ cups and lightly thickened. Stir in the lemon juice, salt, and white pepper. Transfer the sauce to a blender and blend until smooth, about 30 seconds; be careful, because the sauce is very hot. Set aside and keep warm.

To cook the fish, preheat an oven to 450°F. Season the halibut with salt and pepper to taste. Heat the oil in a large, heavy ovenproof skillet over medium-high heat. Cook the fillets until golden brown, about 2 to 3 minutes on each side. Transfer the skillet to the oven and bake the fish until just cooked through, about 3 to 4 minutes, depending on thickness of the fillets.

To serve, ladle ¼ cup of the sauce onto each of 4 warm dinner plates. Place the fillets on top of the sauce and spoon the remaining sauce over them. Garnish with chives.

CHEF'S NOTE: Prized halibut cheeks would be a tasty alternative when available. They range in size from 3 ounces to up to 1 pound each, depending on the size of the fish.

Pacific halibut is found primarily along the North American west coast and is commercially fished mainly off Alaska and British Columbia. In 1923, with stocks suffering from being overfished, the United States and Canada signed a convention on halibut, leading to the creation of the International Pacific Halibut Commission, which today regulates Pacific halibut fishing. Members meet annually to review research, check on the progress of the commercial fishery, and make regulations for the next year's season. This management allows for a maximum of sustained halibut harvesting.

The halibut is the largest of the flatfish and can reach huge proportions. The dream of every angler is to hook a three-hundred-pound fish; you'll often see the halibut sportfisherman having his photo taken while lying next to his catch to show "how big it is." Homer, Alaska, has the longest-running halibut derby—more than twenty years now—with thousands of dollars in prizes for the lucky fisher who brings in the biggest catch.

In 2001, a released-fish prize was added. Larger halibut produce more viable eggs than smaller halibut, so this award recognizes anglers who release a fish of significant breeding potential rather than taking it home. The released-fish entry must be certified by the captain of the boat and signed by the angler; any contestant who catches and releases a halibut over eighty pounds qualifies for the cash drawing.

Halibut is esteemed for its sweet, mild flavor, firm meat, and snow-white color. Market forms of the fish include steaks, fillets, and fletches (split body-length fillets), plus the extra-tasty cheeks so applauded by their culinary fans.

Seafood Risotto San Juan

MAKES 6 TO 8 FIRST-COURSE OR 4 ENTRÉE SERVINGS

The Straits of Juan de Fuca and Georgia and the islands in northern Puget Sound are magnificent getaways. Boaters usually arm themselves with crab traps, fishing poles, and even some scuba gear, since seafood—from crabs to scallops—is plentiful. The ingredients for risotto are easy to stash in your galley—then just add the catch of the day or whatever seafood you like best. Try a Mission Hill pinot grigio or pinot blanc from British Columbia or a Washington sauvignon blanc with this delicate dish.

2 tablespoons extra-virgin olive oil

$3/4$ cup chopped button or chanterelle mushrooms (about 4 ounces)

2 tablespoons minced shallots

1 tablespoon minced fresh garlic

$1^1/2$ cups Arborio rice

$1^1/2$ cups clam juice

$1^1/2$ cups water

$3/4$ cup dry white wine

12 small Manila clams, rinsed

1 tablespoon minced lemon zest

$1/4$ cup minced celery

6 large sea scallops, halved, or $5^1/2$ ounces (1 cup) Dungeness crabmeat

4 squid, cleaned, tubes cut into rings, and tentacles left whole

$1/3$ cup very coarsely grated zucchini, green skin and firm part only, not seedy part

2 tablespoons fresh lemon juice

2 teaspoons minced fresh thyme

3 tablespoons butter, cut into small pieces

$1/2$ cup (2 ounces) grated Parmesan cheese

12 small, red grape tomatoes, halved

Salt

Freshly ground black pepper

Garnishes
Fruity extra-virgin olive oil (optional)
Fresh thyme sprigs
Lemon wedges

In a large, heavy wide saucepan, Dutch oven, or skillet, heat the olive oil over medium-high heat. Sauté the mushrooms and shallots, stirring, for about 2 minutes, or until softened. Stir in the garlic and rice, coating the rice well with the oil, and cook for 2 minutes more to get a little color on the rice.

Meanwhile, in a small saucepan, combine the clam juice and water and bring to a simmer, then turn off the heat.

When the rice is sautéed, stir in the wine and cook, stirring often, until the wine is almost totally absorbed, about 2 minutes.

Stir in $3/4$ cup of the warm clam broth mixture. Simmer the rice slowly, uncovered, stirring often and adjusting the heat as necessary, until the liquid is almost totally absorbed, about 2 minutes. Repeat the process, using another $3/4$ cup of the broth. Repeat again, using another $3/4$ cup of the broth and stirring often; this time it will take about 4 minutes to cook down.

Add the clams, lemon zest, celery, scallops if using, and the remaining $3/4$ cup broth. Simmer slowly, stirring often, until the liquid is almost all absorbed and the clams are just starting to open, about 2 to 3 minutes. Add the squid, crab if using, zucchini, lemon juice, and thyme. Cook about 4 minutes more.

At this time, the squid should be just done, the clams open, and the rice a bit creamy in consistency but al dente (firm to the bite) in the center. Turn off the heat and immediately stir in the butter and cheese. Fold in the tomatoes. Taste the risotto and season as needed with salt and pepper. Discard any clams that do not open.

Divide the risotto among warm bowls, drizzle with olive oil if desired, and garnish with thyme sprigs. Serve with lemon wedges.

CHEF'S NOTE: If you're lucky enough to get your hands on some fresh Oregon truffles, this dish lusts for a generous shaving over the top. And if local sweet corn is in season, you could add ¾ cup of freshly cut kernels at the same time as you add the clams. Never, never make risotto using regular, long-grain white rice; risotto rice—Arborio is the most widely available—will give you that "creamy" texture so key to the dish.

Kathy's Spicy Coconut-Braised Lingcod with Colorful Vegetables

MAKES 4 SERVINGS

The offshore waters near Sitka, Alaska, are rich with a variety of sport fish—from the not-so-pretty-to-look-at but tasty lingcod to the many rockfish species, including Pacific yelloweye, with its giant namesake bulging yellow eyes and bright orange body. (Rockfish are sometimes called snapper in our part of the world.) Any of these would perform well with the subtle flavors of this dish.

2 tablespoons chopped fresh mint

2 tablespoons chopped fresh cilantro

1 cup bean sprouts

1½ teaspoons kosher salt

1 tablespoon sugar

½ teaspoon red pepper flakes

1 tablespoon canola or other vegetable oil

4 thick pieces lingcod (about 1½ pounds total)

1 tablespoon minced peeled fresh ginger

1 tablespoon minced fresh garlic

1 can (13 to 14 ounces) unsweetened coconut milk

1 tablespoon soy sauce

2 tablespoons Asian fish sauce

1 stalk fresh lemongrass, outside pieces stripped off, halved lengthwise, and cut into 3-inch lengths

1 small red bell pepper, cut into thin strips

1 large carrot, julienned

4 green onions, cut into 3-inch pieces

2 tablespoons fresh lime juice

Lime wedges for squeezing

In a medium bowl, toss the mint, cilantro, and bean sprouts and set aside.

In a small bowl, mix the salt, sugar, and pepper flakes. In a large nonstick skillet or sauté pan, heat the oil over medium-high heat. Put the fish on a plate and sprinkle with half the salt mixture. Sear the fish, seasoned-side down, for about 2 minutes, or until browned on the first side. Sprinkle the fish with the remaining salt mixture. Sear for 2 minutes on the second side, moving the fish in the pan as needed to prevent burning.

Add the ginger and garlic and sauté for 20 seconds. Add the coconut milk, soy and fish sauces, lemongrass, bell pepper, carrot, and green onions. Cook for about 5 minutes at a fast simmer, or until the fish is just done and opaque throughout. Stir in the lime juice.

Serve the fish in shallow bowls, ladling the broth and vegetables over the fish. Place a pouf of the sprouts mixture on top. Pass the lime wedges.

CHEF'S NOTE: Serve this fragrant dish with simple bowls of steamed jasmine rice on the side. If lingcod is not available in your area, mahimahi is a good substitute.

Glacier Bay Halibut with Marinated Mussels

MAKES 4 SERVINGS

In addition to taking the lead role, mussels can also be luscious and beautiful supporting players in dishes, adding their unique essence and appearance. One taster of this recipe exclaimed, "I feel like I've died and gone to a restaurant!" This easy, super-sophisticated dish is ideal to make at home for a dinner party. The mussels can be made in advance, so all you have to do is cook the halibut at the last minute.

4 skinless thick-cut halibut fillet portions
   (about 6 ounces each)

Kosher salt

Freshly ground black pepper

1½ tablespoons olive oil

1 leek, white part only, cut into ¼-inch-thick
   slices and thoroughly rinsed

1 to 2 teaspoons water

Marinated Mussels (facing page)

1 tablespoon butter at room temperature

2 teaspoons very finely minced fresh
   rosemary

2 teaspoons minced fresh thyme

Garnish

Fresh thyme sprigs

Preheat an oven to 450°F. Season the halibut on both sides with salt and pepper to taste. Heat 1 tablespoon of the oil in a large, heavy ovenproof skillet over medium-high heat. Cook the halibut on the first side for about 2 to 3 minutes, or until golden. Turn the fillets and cook for about 2 minutes more, or until golden.

Place the pan in the oven and roast the fish until just cooked through, about 3 to 4 minutes, depending on the thickness of the fillets.

Meanwhile, in a large nonstick sauté pan or skillet, heat the remaining ½ tablespoon oil over medium-high heat. Sauté the leek for 30 seconds, then add the water and cook for another 30 seconds, or until the leek is just cooked through.

Add the mussels with their marinade and heat until just warmed through. Remove the pan from the heat and swirl in the butter and minced herbs.

Place each piece of halibut on a warm dinner plate. Divide the leeks and mussels among the plates and drizzle the warm sauce over all. Garnish with a couple of the reserved mussel shells and the thyme sprigs.

Marinated Mussels

1 pound mussels, scrubbed and debearded
    (see page 30)

¼ cup dry white wine, plus more if needed

1½ teaspoons minced shallots

½ teaspoon red pepper flakes

¼ cup Champagne vinegar or
    white wine vinegar

2 teaspoons very finely minced lemon zest

½ cup extra-virgin olive oil

½ teaspoon kosher salt

⅛ teaspoon black pepper

Put the mussels and the ¼ cup wine in a saucepan with a tight-fitting lid. Cover and place over high heat to steam until the mussel shells just open, about 3 minutes. Remove the pan from the heat and let sit, covered, for 30 seconds. Then uncover and let cool. Strain off the mussel juice and measure. Add a little white wine if needed to bring it up to ½ cup. Set aside.

Remove the mussel meats from the shells, discarding any unopened ones, and set the meats aside. (Reserve some of the shells for garnish.)

In a medium bowl, whisk the reserved mussel juice with the remaining ingredients. Add the mussel meats and refrigerate until needed, up to 1 day in advance. (Refrigerate any shells you are using for garnish, too.)

Barbecued Salmon Burgers on Homemade Lemon Dill Buns

MAKES 4 SERVINGS

Grilling doesn't have to be the obligatory hamburgers and hot dogs. How about trying a few new approaches—like salmon burgers! You can serve them topped with different condiments, too, such as the cucumbery yogurt sauce, Raita (page 163), or Tangy Vegetable Slaw (page 65). The bun recipe makes 8 buns, so you can easily double the burger mixture or freeze the extra buns for later use.

Burger Mixture

1½ pounds boneless, skinless salmon fillet, pin bones removed (ask your fishmonger to do this)

½ teaspoon black pepper

1 tablespoon Dijon mustard

2 tablespoons minced onion

1 tablespoon minced fresh dill

1 teaspoon minced fresh garlic

1 tablespoon fresh lemon juice

2 tablespoons dried bread crumbs

¾ teaspoon kosher salt

Lemon Dill Buns (facing page) or high-quality store-bought buns

Mayonnaise or Ultimate Tartar Sauce (page 117)

Any combination of burger goodies that you like, such as tomato, lettuce, onion, or thinly sliced cucumbers for garnishing

To make the burgers, chop the salmon well. Mix it thoroughly with the remaining burger ingredients in a medium bowl. Divide the mixture into 4 portions and shape into 4½- to 5-inch-diameter well-compacted round patties. Refrigerate the patties, tented, for at least 30 minutes or up to overnight to firm.

Prepare a very hot fire in a charcoal grill, or preheat a gas grill to high. The patties are somewhat fragile, so handle carefully. Oil the grill, and set the patties apart on the grill. Cook for about 2 minutes per side, or until nicely marked and just done. Split the buns and toast lightly.

Spread the buns with mayonnaise or tartar sauce, add the burgers, and pile high with garnishes of your choice.

Lemon Dill Buns

MAKES 8 BUNS

½ cup milk

1 tablespoon butter

2 tablespoons sugar

⅓ cup warm water (105° to 115°F)

1 package active dry yeast

2 eggs

½ teaspoon salt

1 tablespoon minced fresh dill

1 tablespoon very finely minced lemon zest

1 tablespoon minced fresh garlic

2½ cups flour

1 tablespoon water

In a small saucepan, bring the milk just to a simmer, remove from the heat, and stir in the butter and sugar. Cool, stirring until lukewarm. Add the warm water and yeast, stirring to dissolve the yeast. Let sit for 5 minutes, or until foamy. Pour the mixture into a large bowl.

Whisk in 1 egg along with the salt, dill, lemon zest, and garlic. Then mix in as much of the flour as needed to make a smooth, moist dough.

Turn out onto a floured surface and knead until smooth, about 6 minutes. Put the dough into a greased large bowl, cover with a damp towel or plastic wrap, and let rise in a warm place until doubled, about 1½ hours.

Preheat an oven to 350°F. Punch down the dough and divide into 8 pieces. Form the pieces into balls and let rest for 10 minutes, covered with a towel. Then press out the balls, flattening into 4-inch-diameter rounds. Place on a greased baking sheet, spaced apart, cover lightly with a towel, and let rise until almost doubled.

In a small bowl, whisk the remaining egg with the 1 tablespoon water. Brush the tops of the buns lightly with the egg wash. Bake for about 20 minutes, or until golden brown.

CHEF'S NOTE: This bun recipe can also be shaped into dinner rolls—exceptional served with a seafood-centered dinner or lunch. Divide the dough into 12 balls, let rise, egg wash, and bake until golden, about 10 to 15 minutes.

MEAT AND POULTRY

Slow-Roasted Martini Short Ribs

MAKES ABOUT 4 SERVINGS

Beef short ribs is a cut of meat that doesn't get as much play as it should on the home dinner table nowadays. A bit old-fashioned but so big-flavored that chefs have rediscovered them, mouth-watering short rib presentations can often be found on fall and winter menus. I decided to try a distinctive preparation with a cocktail take-off . . . hence the title. When served, the ribs are sprinkled with a fun-flavored topping—chopped lemon zest, stuffed green olives, parsley, and cocktail onions—sort of a martini à la gremolata! Fluffy garlic whipped potatoes and an icy martini are the consummate companions to this hearty dish.

4½ to 5 pounds beef short ribs (about 8 pieces)

2 teaspoons salt

½ teaspoon black pepper

2 tablespoons vegetable oil

¼ cup dry white vermouth

¼ cup gin

1¾ cups low-sodium beef broth or homemade beef stock

5 juniper berries, crushed

Topping

1 tablespoon minced lemon zest

¼ cup coarsely chopped pimiento-stuffed green olives

¼ cup coarsely chopped fresh flat-leaf parsley

10 pickled cocktail onions, chopped

2 teaspoons gin

2 tablespoons cornstarch

2 tablespoons cold water

Gin for sprinkling (optional)

Preheat an oven to 325°F. Season the ribs on all sides with the salt and pepper.

In a heavy Dutch oven or large, wide pan with a lid, heat the oil over medium to medium-high heat. Brown the ribs in 2 to 3 batches, for about 2 minutes per side, or until browned on all sides. Transfer the ribs to a plate.

Combine the vermouth, gin, and broth and stir the liquid into the pan. Bring to a simmer and stir to scrape up all the browned bits. Return the ribs to the pan, along with any accumulated juices, and add the juniper berries. Cover and bring just to a boil.

Transfer the pan to the oven and cook for about 2½ hours, or until the meat is tender. (Halfway through the cooking time, rearrange the ribs so that all sides get time in the braising liquid.)

When done, remove the ribs from the pan; pull out the bones, and peel away the connective tissue, if desired. Arrange the meat on a platter and keep warm. Skim the fat from the cooking liquid, then cook to reduce the defatted sauce to about 2 cups.

While the sauce is reducing, make the topping. In a small bowl, mix the lemon zest, olives, parsley, cocktail onions, and gin and set aside. (Or, make ahead and refrigerate until 30 minutes before serving.)

In a separate small bowl, whisk the cornstarch and water to make a slurry, then whisk into the sauce and return to a boil to thicken. Taste the sauce and correct the seasoning if needed. Ladle the sauce over the meat and sprinkle with the topping mixture, and a little gin, if desired.

Is there anything better than biting into a crisp apple on a brisk, sunny fall day? Can't you just hear that snappling, crunchy sound of a really good one?

Though apples are grown all across the Northwest, Washington state has become world-famous for its biggest agricultural crop. Popular history has it that the first apple seed was planted in a Vancouver, Washington, greenhouse about 1825 by Dr. John McLoughlin of the Hudson's Bay Company. In the early twentieth century, with the development of irrigated agriculture east of the Cascades, orchards were planted in the rich, volcanic soil of the interior. The trees took to the sunny days and cool nights, and an industry took root.

Only a few years ago, mellow Red Delicious dominated Washington production, but that's changed quite a lot. People's tastes evolve, and this has brought on a more sophisticated lineup of apples characterized by a sweet-sour tang. With chefs' and consumers' demand for choice, lots of the old favorites have come back, along with plenty of new variations. These days, farmers' markets burgeon with a bounty of heirloom varieties. Though these old-time apples might seem new to the younger set, many locals remember growing up with Winesaps or Jonathans in their backyards.

The long-popular Rome, known for its baking aptitude, has recently met its match in the sweet, firm Cameo and the Fuji, which holds its shape amazingly well when cooked, and my new darling, the Pink Lady.

Another newer variety, the versatile Gala, is a light apple with a perfumey sweet flavor and juicy, creamy flesh under a light-red–pinky-striped exterior, which is delightful for just munching. And still going strong is that bright green standby, Granny Smith, so delish whether baked up in pies or eaten as a crunchy, tart snack. Grannies are also delectable cooked up in a homemade spiced apple relish to dollop on crostini with a slice of artisanal Gouda or to cozy up to a pork roast.

‹ Rosy Washington apples

Sage-Roasted Pork Loin with Apples & Onions

MAKES 6 TO 8 SERVINGS

Pink Lady is the season's last apple harvested in Washington, from late October to November. This unique-tasting pink-blushed apple with creamy crisp flesh adds its super-tangy yet sweet flavor when roasted alongside the sage-rubbed pork.

Rub
6 fresh sage leaves, minced
1½ teaspoons dried thyme leaves
¼ teaspoon red pepper flakes
2 teaspoons kosher salt
1½ tablespoons Dijon mustard
3 tablespoons olive oil

1 boneless pork top loin roast
   (about 2½ pounds)
1½ tablespoons olive oil
3 tablespoons balsamic vinegar
¼ teaspoon kosher salt
2½ pounds unpeeled Pink Lady apples
   (about 4), cut lengthwise into eighths and
   cored, or substitute Gala or Fuji apples
1½ pounds white onions (about 2 medium),
   cut into ½-inch wedges
Fresh sage leaves for garnishing

Preheat an oven to 350°F.

To make the rub and season the pork, mix the rub ingredients well in a small bowl. Pat the pork roast dry with paper towels, then smear the pork on all sides with the rub, using it all. Set the roast on a rimmed baking sheet.

In a large bowl, whisk the oil, vinegar, and salt. Mix in the apples and onions, coating well.

Distribute the apples and onions around the pork and drizzle the marinade over the apples and onions. Roast for about 45 minutes to 1 hour, or until the pork reaches an internal temperature of 160°F and the apples and onions are tender.

Transfer the roast to a platter to rest for 10 minutes before carving. With a spoon, move the apples and onions around in the baking pan to coat them with pan juices. Serve the pork, sliced, with the apples, onions, and juice spooned over it. Garnish with sage leaves.

Mustard-Rubbed Lamb Rack with Apple Mint "Marmalade"

MAKES 4 SERVINGS

Local lamb is enjoyed all over the Northwest, and this preparation pairs it with two other major crops, apples and mint. In fact, Washington and Oregon are the top mint-producers in the United States. This homemade condiment should persuade the most ardent devotee of store-bought mint jelly to try something new. Merlot is the "must-do" wine pairing with lamb.

2 Frenched racks of lamb (about 2½ pounds total), cracked between the ribs for easy carving

Rub

3 tablespoons whole-grain mustard

2 tablespoons prepared horseradish

2 teaspoons kosher salt

1 teaspoon coarsely ground black pepper

4 cloves garlic, minced or pressed through a garlic press

1 tablespoon minced fresh thyme

1 tablespoon olive oil

Marmalade

1 tablespoon butter

1 unpeeled, large green apple, cored and coarsely grated

1 tablespoon cider vinegar

½ cup red pepper jelly

1 tablespoon minced fresh mint

Garnish

Fresh mint sprigs

There should be only a thin layer of fat remaining over the meaty side of the lamb ribs. If the fat is too thick, trim it carefully with a sharp knife.

To make the rub, mix the ingredients in a small bowl until a paste is formed. Dry the lamb well with paper towels, then smear the paste on the meaty parts of the lamb, dividing it evenly between the two racks and using all the rub. Let sit at room temperature for about 20 minutes while you make the marmalade.

To make the marmalade, melt the butter in a medium skillet or sauté pan over medium-high heat. Sauté the apple for about 4 to 5 minutes, or until just tender. Add the vinegar, pepper jelly, and mint and bring to a boil. Let the mixture boil for about 2 minutes, until loose and chutney-like. Remove from the heat and let cool.

Meanwhile, preheat an oven to 450°F. Set the lamb racks in a shallow roasting pan, placing them on the flat, bony side with the Frenched rib bones standing up. Roast the lamb to an internal temperature of 130°F for medium-rare, or to the doneness you like. Allow about 15 to 18 minutes for medium-rare.

Remove the racks from the oven and loosely tent with foil; let stand for 5 minutes before carving so the juices don't run out. (The internal temperature will increase by about 5°F as the meat rests.) Carve each rack into chops, cutting between the bones.

Serve 3 to 4 chops per person. Dollop a spoonful of marmalade onto each serving and garnish with mint sprigs.

CHEF'S NOTE: Accompany with "Green" Rice Prima Vera with Asparagus, Peas & Pods (page 186) or roasted fingerling potatoes and sautéed green beans with shallots.

Farm-direct juicy Bing cherries

Almond Chicken with Sassy Bing Cherry Salsa

MAKES 4 SERVINGS

Our local Bing cherries make a sprightly salsa, their sweetness set off agreeably by the tart and spicy elements. This salsa is also a winning choice to top simply grilled or pan-seared salmon.

2 tablespoons flour

1½ teaspoons salt

2 teaspoons ground coriander

¼ teaspoon cayenne pepper

4 large boneless, skinless chicken
　breast halves

2 tablespoons butter

½ cup (2 ounces) sliced almonds

¼ cup dry white wine

Sassy Bing Cherry Salsa (recipe follows)

Cilantro sprigs for garnishing

Preheat an oven to 375°F.

In a shallow bowl, mix the flour, salt, coriander, and cayenne. Dredge the chicken breasts in the flour mixture, shaking off the excess. Set aside.

In a large, ovenproof nonstick skillet, melt 1 tablespoon of the butter over medium-high heat. Brown the chicken lightly on each side for about 1 minute. Lay the chicken in the pan, sprinkle with the almonds, and place the pan in the oven. Cook the chicken until the juices run clear, about 6 to 10 minutes, depending on the thickness of the meat. Transfer the chicken and almonds to a warm platter and keep warm. (Reserve the pan for next step.)

Return the pan to medium-high heat, add the wine, and bring to a simmer, stirring to scrape up all the browned bits in the pan. Add the remaining 1 tablespoon butter and whisk until slightly reduced and thickened.

Spoon the sauce over the chicken and top with the cherry salsa. Garnish with cilantro sprigs.

Sassy Bing Cherry Salsa

MAKES ABOUT 2 CUPS

2 cups pitted sliced Bing cherries
　(about 1 pound)

2 tablespoons seasoned rice vinegar

¼ cup minced Walla Walla Sweet onion or
　other sweet white onion

1 tablespoon finely chopped fresh cilantro

1½ teaspoons very finely minced peeled
　fresh ginger

¼ to ½ teaspoon red pepper flakes
　(depending on how spicy you like it)

In a small bowl, gently mix all the ingredients. The salsa is best if made right before serving but can be made up to 2 hours in advance.

Chicken Parmesan Penne Bake with Fresh Herbs & Artichokes

MAKES 6 TO 8 SERVINGS

Combining ingredients everyone loves, this entrée will comfort the crowd as well as the host. Try making it with a combination of artisanal cheeses.

4 tablespoons (½ stick) butter

2 tablespoons olive oil

1½ pounds boneless, skinless chicken
    breasts, cut into 1-inch pieces

1½ teaspoons salt

¼ teaspoon black pepper

2 cups sliced cremini mushrooms
    (about 10 ounces)

2 tablespoons minced fresh garlic

⅛ teaspoon cayenne pepper

6 tablespoons flour

5 cups milk

1 pound dried penne pasta

1 can (about 14 ounces) artichoke hearts,
    drained and coarsely chopped

1 tablespoon minced fresh thyme

2 tablespoons finely chopped fresh basil

2 tablespoons thinly sliced fresh chives

2 cups (8 ounces) shredded mozzarella cheese

1 cup (4 ounces) grated Parmesan cheese

Preheat an oven to 375°F. Lightly butter a 9-by-13-inch baking pan or dish or spray with vegetable-oil cooking spray.

In a large, heavy skillet, melt the butter with the oil over medium-high heat. Sauté the chicken, sprinkling with the salt and pepper, for about 3 minutes, until the chicken turns opaque. Add the mushrooms and cook for 2 minutes more, or until the mushrooms are limp. Add the garlic and cayenne and stir for about 20 seconds; do not let the garlic brown. Whisk in the flour and cook for 1 minute, stirring constantly. Immediately add the milk, whisking vigorously. Bring to a simmer and cook, whisking occasionally, for about 6 minutes, or until the sauce is thickened. Remove from the heat and set aside to let cool slightly.

Meanwhile, in a large pot of salted boiling water, cook the pasta according to package directions, or until just al dente. Drain well.

In a very large bowl, mix the pasta and sauce. Fold in the artichokes, herbs, mozzarella, and ¾ cup of the Parmesan until well combined. Spread the mixture in the prepared baking dish. Sprinkle with the remaining ¼ cup Parmesan and bake for about 25 to 30 minutes, or until the pasta is heated through, the sides are slightly bubbling, and the top is golden brown.

Fan Tan Duck Breast with Blackberries

MAKES 4 SERVINGS

Pheasants, quail, and especially duck are found in the Northwest hunter's freezer. Duck is often prepared with berries, apples, or dried prunes. Named after the famous alley in the heart of Canada's oldest Chinatown in Victoria, British Columbia, this recipe incorporates the Chinese spice star anise, a fun flavor-pairing with blackberries.

Marinade

1 orange, quartered

2 tablespoons raspberry vinegar

1/4 cup sake

2 tablespoons soy sauce

2 star anise pods, crushed

6 black peppercorns, crushed

4 slices unpeeled fresh ginger, crushed

4 large cloves garlic, crushed

4 boneless duck breast halves, about
   6 ounces each

Salt

1 tablespoon blackberry or other honey

2 teaspoons cornstarch

1/2 cup low-sodium chicken broth or
   homemade chicken stock

1 cup fresh or frozen blackberries

Whole fresh chives for garnishing

CHEF'S NOTE: Baked sweet potatoes, wild rice pilaf, or Rosemary Roasted Squash (page 178) would be an outstanding accompaniment.

To make the marinade, squeeze the orange quarters into a medium bowl, then drop in the pieces. Mix in the remaining marinade ingredients.

With a sharp knife, score the duck skin and fat, not quite all the way through to the meat, at 1/2-inch intervals in two directions to form a diamond pattern. Dredge the duck in the marinade, turning to coat thoroughly, then marinate for 4 hours or up to overnight, refrigerated, turning the pieces occasionally.

When ready to cook the duck, preheat an oven to 425°F and have all the remaining ingredients ready within reach of the stove.

Remove the duck from the marinade and pat dry on all sides with paper towels. Season the skin side lightly with salt. Reserve the marinade.

Heat a large, ovenproof nonstick skillet or sauté pan over medium-high heat until hot. Sear the duck breasts, skin-side down, for 1 1/2 minutes. Turn and sear on the meat side for 1 1/2 to 2 minutes. Transfer the duck to a plate. Drain off the accumulated duck fat. Return the duck to the hot skillet, skin-side down, and put the pan in the oven. Roast the duck for 8 to 10 minutes, or until skin is crispy and duck is cooked.

Meanwhile, strain the marinade, pressing on the solids to get all the juice. Whisk in the honey. In a separate small bowl, whisk the cornstarch into the chicken broth to make a slurry.

Remove the duck from the pan (remember, the handle is hot—use a pot holder!) and keep warm. Carefully drain the accumulated fat, then set the pan on a burner over high heat. Stir in the strained marinade, scraping up all the browned bits, and bring it to a simmer. Whisk the slurry again, then whisk it into the simmering sauce. Return the sauce to a simmer and cook to reduce it for 3 to 4 minutes, whisking frequently. Add the berries and any accumulated juices from the duck, and simmer until saucy and berries are heated through.

To serve, slice each duck breast on the diagonal into 8 slices, arrange on serving plates, and spoon the sauce and berries over the duck. Garnish with chives.

WILD MUSHROOMING: TREASURE HUNTING IN THE NORTHWEST

Mushrooming's the compleat Northwest outdoor sport. These aren't little wooded paths that foragers take to find the elusive wild fungi; these are hikes into the deep of the woods. It's a workout plowing over fallen trees and rough terrain, but it's worth it to see a chanterelle's orange head pushing up from a blanket of fuzzy moss or bed of Douglas fir needles. It's a thrill just like treasure hunting, and when you find a big patch, it's like hitting the jackpot!

Predicting where and when these jewels will emerge is an art. Key elements are timing, temperature, and elevation, and there are biological indicators, such as the appearance of other plants and flowers blooming.

Come early spring, people head out to look for the first signs of morels. A charge rushes through you as you see a tiny black or brown head, camouflaged by fallen leaves, bark, or burned forest remains, peeking out of the ground. Or if you're really lucky, you find a six- to ten-inch monster morel staring you right in the face, just standing there like a perky little Christmas tree. All 'shroomers lust after the true morel, the *Morchella sp.* The name given to the variety in this region is *Morchella elata*. Look for these on the eastern side of the Cascades on south-facing slopes in April and May and then on north-facing slopes as the season progresses into June or even August.

In the fall, after the rains return, you might find the gigantic cauliflower mushroom that grows on stumps, chanterelles, brilliant red lobster mushrooms, boletes, or the perfumey, matsutake coveted by Japanese cooks. *Boletus edulis,* called the king bolete, is known as *porcino* in Italian or *cèpe* in French. This mushroom is loved for its robust flavor as well as its meaty texture. Chanterelles occur in second-growth forests from as early as August to as late as Thanksgiving, depending on the first big frost.

'Shroomers are very secretive about their "spots." Why? With much habitat being destroyed by logging and development, many species are more difficult to find every year.

When preparing edible wild mushrooms, it is very important to cook them thoroughly. Some undesirable compounds are broken down by heat and cooking also enhances the flavor of mushrooms and releases their nutritional elements. Wild mushrooms are splendid simply sautéed in a little butter or olive oil with some garlic, then deglazed with a splash of white wine and tossed with a few fresh herbs. And many ordinary dishes can be zipped up a few notches by the addition of wild mushrooms—for example, sautéed and folded into mashed potatoes, scattered over scrumptious eggs Benedict with crab, or added to oyster stew. Sautéed and marinated wild mushrooms are regularly seen on restaurant menus in luscious warm mushroom salads with local greens.

Just remember, if you're foraging, that there are many poisonous mushrooms. Be sure of what you're picking. Hunt with an experienced mushroom-picking friend, or join a mycological society and link up with one of their field trips (see page 224).

Soy, Ginger & Sake Beef Pot Roast with Shiitakes

MAKES 6 TO 8 SERVINGS

Pot roast is an old standby, and slow braising brings out its rich flavor and succulent tenderness. The fall-off-your-fork, Japanese-flavor-infused beef and tender mushrooms are wonderful escorted by simple steamed potatoes or jasmine rice and Zingy Cucumber Salad (page 90). Serve this with small glasses of sake or chilled bottles of Japanese beer, such as Sapporo.

2 tablespoons vegetable oil

1 beef chuck (pot) roast (4 pounds)

1 cup sake

1 large white onion, cut into
    ½-inch-thick slices

4 cloves fresh garlic

2-inch piece unpeeled fresh ginger, washed
    well and cut into ¼-inch-thick slices

2 tablespoons sugar

¼ cup soy sauce

18 small shiitake mushrooms, stemmed

3 tablespoons cornstarch

3 tablespoons cold water

3 green onions, thinly sliced, for garnishing

Preheat an oven to 325°F. In a heavy Dutch oven or other large, wide pan with a lid, heat the oil over medium to medium-high heat. Sear the meat until nicely browned, about 2 to 3 minutes per side. (When meat is browned on the first side, it should be easy to turn.)

Stir the sake into the pan, scraping up all the browned bits. Add the onion, garlic, and ginger. In a small bowl, dissolve the sugar in the soy sauce and pour over the meat. Add the mushrooms, cover the pan, and bring just to a boil.

Transfer the pan to the oven and cook for about 3 hours, or until the meat is tender. Turn the roast over in the liquid about halfway through the cooking time.

Carefully transfer the meat to a platter and place the drained mushrooms and onion around and on top of the meat. Set aside and keep warm. Skim the fat from the sauce if needed, then return the pan to a burner and bring the sauce to a boil. Boil for 2 minutes to reduce the volume and intensify flavors.

Meanwhile, in a small bowl, whisk the cornstarch and water to make a slurry, then whisk into the sauce. Return to a boil to thicken, whisking constantly. Taste the sauce and correct the seasoning if needed.

Sprinkle the green onions over the meat and serve the sauce on the side.

CHEF'S NOTE: For a low-carb version, omit the sugar from the recipe. Instead of thickening with the cornstarch slurry, remove the meat and mushrooms from the pan, then cook to reduce the liquid until saucy.

Chili & Lime Slow-Cooked Pork with Red Onion Escabeche and Warm Tortillas

MAKES 6 HEARTY SERVINGS

Mexican and other Latin American culinary influences are numerous in the Northwest, especially in eastern Oregon and Washington, where entrepreneurial immigrants have brought the bold flavors of their foods to taquerias, restaurants, and bakeries. This dish is also a primo appetizer: coarsely chop the cooked pork, pan-sear, then pile it on crisped mini tortillas. Try it with the Sunset Sage Margarita (page 36).

Pork

¼ cup chili powder

1 tablespoon coriander seed, crushed

1 tablespoon salt

1 boneless pork butt (shoulder), about
   3 pounds, cut into 2 pieces

2 large tomatoes, chopped

4 cloves garlic, sliced

¼ cup fresh lime juice

Escabeche

2 large carrots, julienned

1 large red onion, thinly sliced

½ cup fresh lime juice

2 tablespoons corn or other vegetable oil

½ cup coarsely chopped fresh cilantro
   (about 1 bunch)

1 teaspoon salt

Accompaniments

Warm corn tortillas

Sour cream

Salsa or freshly made pico de gallo

Queso fresco (Mexican-style fresh cheese)

Fresh cilantro sprigs

Lime wedges

To prepare the pork, mix the chili powder, coriander seed, and salt in a large, shallow bowl. Roll the pork in the mixture, taking up all the seasoning.

Put the pork in a slow-cooker, add the remaining ingredients, and set the cooker on high. Let cook for 8 hours—or up to 10 hours if you're still at work!

When ready to serve, mix the escabeche ingredients well, then place in a serving dish. Shred the pork and place in a large serving bowl with some of the cooking liquid.

Serve the pork with the escabeche and accompaniments. Diners build their own "soft tacos," then squeeze lime juice over the filling before folding.

CHEF'S NOTE: To heat tortillas, place them, one by one, on a dry skillet over medium-high heat and turn frequently. As they are heated, slip them between the folds of a clean dish towel or cloth napkin. Wrap the towel in foil (or put into a small casserole dish and cover) to steam the tortillas in their own heat and moisture. Or, microwave the tortillas very briefly and put into a napkin as above. Or, wrap several tortillas in a foil packet and steam them in a steamer until just heated through; use directly from the foil or wrap in a towel as described above.

WINE

Each region of the Northwest's rapidly expanding wine industry is known for its distinctive varietals. Washington state, with more than 360 wineries, is the second largest premium-wine producer in the United States. The majority of Washington's grapes are grown in the cold-winter, hot-summer desert environment east of the Cascade Mountains, where Yakima and Columbia Valleys' viticultural areas make up 94 percent of the state's total wine-grape acreage. Washington is known worldwide for its marvelous red wines, from velvety merlots with sweet cherry–berry notes and complex aromas to big bold cabernets, spicy syrahs, and aromatic cabernet francs. White varietals include crisp chardonnay, semillon, sauvignon blanc, Gewürztraminer, Riesling, and viognier.

In Oregon, there are more than three hundred wineries, and the vintage is drawn from several distinct regions. The north and south Willamette Valley appellations taken together are the state's largest, stretching from Portland to Eugene, more than one hundred miles to the south. Most of the wineries are concentrated in this location as well. In contrast to 75 percent of Washington's vineyard plantings, Oregon's wine-growing areas are west of the Cascades, where summer temperatures are lower than in the more arid interior. This cooler climate is perfect for growing early-ripening pinot noir grapes, which go into producing the bright and fruity, rich and mysterious nuances of the wines for which Oregon is internationally noted. Other Oregon varietals include pinot gris, Riesling, and chardonnay.

The smaller, younger premium-wine regions in British Columbia stretch across the province. The Okanagan Valley and Similkameen Valley designated viticultural areas are in the warmer and drier rain shadow east of the Cascades. Vancouver Island and Fraser Valley are milder and moister regions in southwestern British Columbia. The strength of that province's wine portfolio is displayed in its whites: pinot blanc, pinot gris, chardonnay, Riesling, and semillon. But it's most known for its ice wines and late-harvest dessert wines.

Beef Stroganoff with Pinot Noir & Garlic Parsley Noodles

MAKES 4 SERVINGS

Oregon is known for its pinot noir. The wine's characteristic notes of blackberry, chocolate, and spice give full flavor to this updated classic dish. If you ever have the chance to snatch up a bottle of Domaine Drouhin Oregon pinot, do it—it is my absolutely most-loved Oregon wine.

Parsley Butter

4 tablespoons (½ stick) butter, softened

1 teaspoon minced fresh garlic

¼ cup minced fresh parsley

½ teaspoon salt

2 tablespoons sour cream

Beef

3 tablespoons olive oil

1¼ pounds beef tenderloin, cut into
   ½-by-2-inch strips

¾ teaspoon salt

¼ teaspoon black pepper

1 cup thinly sliced red onion

1½ cups sliced mushrooms (about 8 ounces)

¾ cup dry red wine, such as an
   Oregon pinot noir

1½ teaspoons Worcestershire sauce

1 cup low-sodium beef broth or homemade
   beef stock

2 teaspoons cornstarch

¾ cup sour cream

Salt

12 ounces dried broad egg noodles

Garnishes

Sour cream

Fresh flat-leaf parsley sprigs

Put a pot of water on the stove and bring to a simmer. Cover until ready to cook the noodles.

To make the parsley butter, combine all the ingredients in a food processor and purée until smooth, then set aside.

To cook the beef, heat 2 tablespoons of the oil in a very large nonstick sauté pan over medium-high heat. Add the beef strips and sprinkle with salt and pepper. Sauté for about 4 to 5 minutes, until the beef is lightly browned on the outside and about three-quarters cooked. With a slotted spoon, transfer the beef to a plate and set aside, keeping the pan on the heat.

Add the remaining 1 tablespoon oil to the pan, then the onion and mushrooms. Stirring often, cook for about 2 to 4 minutes, until the onion is tender. Add the wine, increase the heat to high, and cook until the wine is almost totally evaporated, about 4 to 6 minutes.

Meanwhile, in a small bowl, mix the Worcestershire, broth, and cornstarch until smooth. When the wine has evaporated, add the mixture to the pan and bring to a boil. The sauce should thicken slightly. Stir in the sour cream, then the reserved beef. Cook until heated through, but do not let the sauce boil.

Meanwhile, bring the pot of water to a boil, add salt, and cook the noodles according to package directions just until tender. Drain well, return to the cooking pot, and stir in the parsley butter to coat the noodles well.

Divide the noodles among individual pasta bowls and top with the beef and sauce. Garnish each serving with a dollop of sour cream and a parsley sprig.

CHEF'S NOTE: If making this recipe with a homemade stock, you will need to add salt to taste.

Herb-Lacquered Chicken with Red Wine Cranberry Compote

MAKES 4 TO 6 SERVINGS

Fresh herbs tucked under the skin not only add splendid flavor but also make this dish a real showstopper, as the translucent skin becomes lacquered during cooking—for the most gorgeous roasted chicken ever. Try this method on your holiday turkey as well. And either bird would be set off by a bottle of DeLille Cellars' D2, a Bordeaux-style red wine replete with complex, mouth-filling fruit flavors.

1 large (4-pound) roasting chicken, preferably organic or free-range

2 unpeeled cloves garlic, halved

4 small fresh rosemary sprigs

4 large fresh sage leaves

4 fresh thyme sprigs

1 tablespoon butter, melted

1 tablespoon soy sauce

½ teaspoon kosher salt

¼ teaspoon freshly ground black pepper

Red Wine Cranberry Compote (page 152)

Preheat an oven to 425°F. Spray a roasting rack with vegetable-oil cooking spray.

Remove the neck and any giblets from the chicken cavity. Rinse the chicken with cold water inside and out, and pat dry. Put the garlic in the body cavity.

Carefully loosen the chicken skin over the breast and legs by running your hands under it, being careful not to tear it. Keeping the leaves as flat as possible, tuck the rosemary, sage, and thyme under the breast, thigh, and leg skin, arranging the herbs decoratively. Carefully pull the breast skin tightly down over the breastbone. Tuck the wings under and tie the legs together with kitchen twine. Place the chicken on the prepared roasting rack and set on a rimmed baking sheet.

In a small bowl, mix the butter and soy sauce. Brush the chicken all over with the mixture, then sprinkle with the salt and pepper.

Roast the chicken for about 45 minutes, or until the inner, thickest part of the thigh registers 160°F on an instant-read thermometer inserted in the back side of thigh by the body. Remove from the oven and let rest for 10 minutes to allow the juices to settle before carving.

The chicken is beautiful presented on a platter and carved at the table. Pass the compote separately.

Continued›

CHEF'S NOTE: To make a little sauce to drizzle over the chicken, pour off the excess fat from the baking sheet. Stir in ½ cup fruity, dry red wine and 1 tablespoon water, set the pan over medium heat, and stir to scrape up the browned pan drippings. Cook to reduce to half, then taste and adjust the seasoning.

Red Wine Cranberry Compote

MAKES ABOUT 2½ CUPS

¾ cup dry red wine

½ cup finely chopped onion

1 tablespoon minced peeled fresh ginger

1 unpeeled large Gala apple, cored and
    cut into ¼-inch dice

One 12-ounce bag (3 cups) fresh or frozen
    cranberries, chopped

½ cup orange juice

1 cup sugar

¼ teaspoon ground cloves

¼ teaspoon ground cinnamon

In a medium nonreactive saucepan, combine all the ingredients. Bring to a simmer over medium-high heat, reduce the heat to medium, and simmer for about 30 to 35 minutes, or until thickened and chutney-like in consistency. The mixture will thicken a little more after cooling. Serve warm or at room temperature.

CHEF'S NOTE: The compote keeps, refrigerated, for up to 7 days and is fine on sandwiches and with roasted turkey and pork, also.

Pan-Seared Venison with Port & Oregon Blue Cheese Sauce

MAKES 4 SERVINGS

Although the term venison *refers today to the meat of antlered animals such as deer, elk, antelope, reindeer, and moose, most of the venison eaten now is deer. Some animals have an exceptional diet from "browsing" in accessible backyards, eating the sweet new rosebuds and nipping off the tender young sprouts and leaves of fruit trees. Venison is somewhat similar to beef except that it is very lean; it can be successfully cooked as you would beef. Accompany this venison dish with Savory Chanterelle Bread Pudding (page 176) or Walla Walla "French Onion" Mashed Potatoes (page 175) and sautéed Brussels sprouts.*

1½ pounds venison, such as loin or
    tenderloin, cut into 8 to 12 medallions

Kosher salt

Freshly ground black pepper

1 tablespoon clarified butter or olive oil,
    plus more if needed

1 shallot, minced

2 large fresh sage leaves

¾ cup port wine

1 tablespoon Dijon mustard

½ cup demi-glace (see Chef's Note)
    or low-sodium beef broth

3 tablespoons heavy whipping cream

½ cup crumbled Oregon blue cheese or other
    full-flavored blue cheese (about 2 ounces)

Garnishes

Fresh sage leaves

Crumbled blue cheese

A few fresh huckleberries if in season

CHEF'S NOTE: Rarely does anyone ever make demi-glace, a super-reduced veal stock, at home anymore because there are superlative alternatives. I recommend More Than Gourmet Demi-Glace Gold (see page 223).

Preheat an oven to 140° to 145°F. (If your oven thermostat is not marked this low, use an oven thermometer, preheat the oven on the lowest setting, then turn off the heat.) Have all ingredients ready within reach of the range.

Between sheets of plastic wrap, lightly pound the medallions with a meat mallet or the heel of your hand to flatten out slightly. Season each medallion with salt and pepper on all sides.

In a large, heavy nonstick skillet or sauté pan, heat the clarified butter over high heat. (If you do not have a pan large enough to sear all the venison at one time, uncrowded, work in batches or use two pans.) Sear the medallions for 1½ to 2 minutes per side for medium-rare. (Be sure to cook the venison quickly in a very hot pan.)

Set the seared pieces of venison on a wire rack set on a baking sheet in the low oven. When all the meat is seared, stir the shallot and sage leaves into the pan, cooking for about 30 seconds, then stir in the port and mustard and scrape up the browned bits in the bottom of the pan to get all that good flavor into the sauce. Continue to cook on high heat to reduce the port to ¼ cup, about 1½ minutes. Whisk in the demi-glace and cream and reduce until saucy and almost glossy, about 3½ to 4 minutes. Add the cheese and whisk in for about 30 seconds to 1 minute, then remove the sauce from heat.

Remove and discard the sage leaves. Whisk in any accumulated juices from the venison, taste the sauce, and adjust the seasoning with salt and pepper if needed.

To serve, arrange the venison on dinner plates and drizzle with the sauce, dividing evenly. Garnish with the fresh sage leaves and a sprinkling of cheese and huckleberries.

Garlic Gulch Braised Rabbit Ragù with Pappardelle Pasta

MAKES 6 TO 8 FIRST-COURSE OR 4 ENTRÉE SERVINGS

Northwest family rabbit stories proliferate like rabbits. A man who grew up in the 1960s in Seattle's Rainier Valley, then an Italian-American neighborhood nicknamed Garlic Gulch, tells this weird tale. His father, his brother, and he would take the ferry over to Lopez Island, where they would drive the car out into a field. After the sun had gone down and the moon was casting its glow, the boys would lie on the hood with their feet tied to the car so they wouldn't fall off, and the father would drive slowly through the field with the headlights on. Any passing rabbits would be mesmerized by the car lights, and the boys would reach down and pick up the glassy-eyed rabbits by the ears. Back at home, the game was braised in a robust stew with lots of garlic and red wine. This version is not as strenuous to make!

1 tablespoon extra-virgin olive oil, plus more
    for drizzling
Kosher salt
1 pound fresh pasta sheets, such as egg with
    parsley, or substitute fettuccine pasta
Braised Rabbit Ragù (facing page)

Garnishes
Freshly shaved Parmigiano-Reggiano (see
    page 28) or grana cheese
Fresh thyme sprigs

Bring 2 gallons of water to a boil in a large pot over high heat. Add the 1 tablespoon oil and a big pinch of salt.

Meanwhile, cut the pasta sheets (if using) into 1-inch-wide strips and fluff with your hands to separate. A few strips at a time, drop the pasta into the boiling water and stir to separate; keep a close eye on the pasta while cooking to be sure that the pieces do not stick together. Cook the pasta until just al dente, about 2 to 4 minutes, then immediately drain well. Do not rinse. Put the pasta in a large bowl, drizzle with a little oil, sprinkle with salt, and toss to coat. Mix in 1 cup ragù.

Divide the pasta among large, shallow pasta bowls, and top with the remaining sauce. Drizzle with oil if desired. Shave cheese to taste over each portion and garnish with thyme.

Braised Rabbit Ragù

2 pounds rabbit, cut into serving pieces,
    then bigger pieces halved or quartered
1 teaspoon kosher salt
¼ teaspoon black pepper
3 tablespoons olive oil
½ cup diced onion
⅓ cup diced parsnip
⅓ cup diced celery
⅓ cup diced carrot
3 tablespoons minced fresh garlic
3 tablespoons tomato paste
1 cup dry red wine
2 bay leaves
2 large fresh rosemary sprigs
1 tablespoon minced fresh thyme
1 cup low-sodium chicken broth or
    homemade chicken stock
1 can (28 ounces) plum tomatoes in juice

Season the rabbit all over with the salt and pepper. Reserve the rabbit liver (if available) in the refrigerator.

In a large braising pan or Dutch oven, heat the oil over medium-high heat. Brown the rabbit pieces for about 2 minutes on each side. (Do not crowd the pan; brown the rabbit in batches if necessary.) As the rabbit is browned, transfer to a plate.

When all the rabbit is browned, add the onion, parsnip, celery, and carrot to the same pan and sauté for about 3 minutes, or until the vegetables are tender. Stir in the garlic and tomato paste and sauté for 1 minute. Add the wine and cook to reduce for 5 minutes, stirring to scrape up the browned bits. Add the bay leaves, rosemary, thyme, and broth. Using your clean hands, "squish" the tomatoes and add them to the mixture with their juice.

Return the rabbit and any accumulated juices to the pan. Make sure the rabbit is covered with the liquid. Bring to a simmer and braise, uncovered, keeping the sauce at a constant low simmer for 50 to 60 minutes, or until the meat is thoroughly tender.

Remove the sauce from the heat and transfer the rabbit meat from the sauce to a baking sheet. Discard the bay leaves and rosemary. Finely chop the reserved liver (if using) and stir into the hot sauce.

When the meat is cool enough to handle, pull the meat from the bones. Discard the bones, chop the meat into rustic pieces, and mix it back into the sauce. (Be careful of little tiny bones.) Taste the sauce for salt and adjust the seasoning if needed. Serve hot.

CHEF'S NOTE: You can make the sauce up to 3 days ahead, then let cool and refrigerate. The ragù is also excellent served over soft polenta.

Backyard Grilled Flank Steak with Feta Cheese & Summer Veggies
with Oregano-Lemon-Olive Vinaigrette

I guess that, in some locales, it need not be summer to make this dish, but in the Northwest we do like to keep our grills busy when it's sunny outside. You can grill the veggies first, as they are just as enjoyable served warm or at room temperature.

Steak and Marinade

1 flank steak (1½ to 2 pounds)

⅓ cup pitted kalamata olives

½ teaspoon kosher salt

½ teaspoon coarsely ground black pepper

1 tablespoon minced fresh garlic

2 tablespoons olive oil

¼ cup dry red wine

Topping

¼ cup pitted kalamata olives, chopped

⅓ cup ¼-inch-diced white onion

2 tablespoons coarsely chopped fresh
   flat-leaf parsley

1 teaspoon minced fresh garlic

3 tablespoons extra-virgin olive oil

Kosher salt

Freshly ground black pepper

Summer Veggies with Oregano-Lemon-Olive
   Vinaigrette (page 158)

About ½ cup crumbled feta cheese

Leaves of fresh flat-leaf parsley

Fresh oregano sprigs for garnishing

To marinate the steak, trim the meat of any outer pieces of fat and silver skin. Put the steak in a large resealable plastic bag.

In a food processor or blender, combine the marinade ingredients and process until puréed. Pour the marinade into the plastic bag, press out any air, then seal the bag. Move the meat around in the bag to coat meat well. Marinate, refrigerated, for at least 1 hour or preferably overnight, turning the bag a few times.

To grill the steak, prepare a medium-hot fire in a charcoal grill, or preheat a gas grill to medium-high. Remove the steak from the marinade and drain well. Discard the marinade.

Mix the topping ingredients and set aside. Have the salt, pepper, and remaining ingredients ready.

Sprinkle the steak with salt and pepper and grill for about 4 to 6 minutes per side, for medium-rare, or cook to the desired doneness. The grilling time will vary, depending on the heat of the grill and the thickness of the meat. Flank steak is most tender when grilled to rare or medium-rare.

Let the steak rest for about 5 minutes before serving, allowing juices to settle. Thinly slice on the diagonal, across the grain. Keeping the slices together, transfer them to a clean, warm platter. Spoon any juices onto the meat. Stir the reserved topping mixture once more, then pour it over the slices.

Arrange the summer veggies on the platter, then scatter the meat and vegetables with the feta and parsley leaves. Garnish with oregano sprigs.

Continued›

Summer Veggies with Oregano-Lemon-Olive Vinaigrette

MAKES 6 SERVINGS

Vinaigrette

1¹/₂ teaspoons minced lemon zest

1 tablespoon fresh lemon juice

1 teaspoon minced fresh oregano

1 teaspoon minced fresh garlic

1 teaspoon Dijon mustard

¹/₄ cup olive oil

8 pitted kalamata olives, very finely chopped

Veggies

1 large red bell pepper, cut lengthwise into
   6 wedges and seeded

1 zucchini, cut into ¹/₂-inch-thick long
   diagonal slices

1 yellow crookneck squash, cut into
   ¹/₂-inch-thick long diagonal slices

2 large portobello mushrooms, stemmed
   and cut into 3 pieces each

1 large eggplant, cut into ¹/₂-inch-thick
   crosswise rounds

Olive oil for grilling

Kosher salt

Cracked black pepper

Prepare a hot fire in a charcoal grill, or preheat a gas grill to high.

To make the vinaigrette, whisk the lemon zest and juice, oregano, garlic, and mustard in a small bowl, then gradually drizzle in the oil, whisking until emulsified. Stir in the olives. Set aside.

Lay the vegetables on a baking sheet and drizzle or brush with oil. Season lightly with salt and pepper to taste. Turn the vegetable slices, then drizzle and season again.

Grill the vegetables for about 1 to 3 minutes on each side to grill-mark nicely. Move the vegetables to a cooler area of the grill and cook, turning occasionally, until just done to your taste. Allow about 3 to 4 minutes total for the bell pepper; about 4 to 6 minutes for the zucchini, yellow squash, and mushrooms; and about 6 to 8 minutes for the eggplant. For the firmer vegetables, you might want to cover them loosely with foil or the grill lid for a few minutes of the cooking time so that the centers get tender all the way through.

As the vegetables are done, transfer them from the grill to a large platter and drizzle generously with the vinaigrette.

Pan-Roasted Spiced Chicken with Fresh Figs & Port

MAKES 6 SERVINGS

Fresh figs are out of this world in this dish but so are Italian plums, which grow effortlessly in Northwest backyards. Just substitute a dozen large ripe plums, pitted and quartered, for the figs. And you might want to grace this dish with a Washington port, such as Willow Crest's nonvintage syrah port or Wind River Cellars' traditional-port-style wine made with rich Lemberger fruit from the famous Celilo Vineyard.

2 teaspoons ground coriander

1 teaspoon ground cardamom

1 teaspoon black pepper

¼ teaspoon cayenne pepper

1 tablespoon kosher salt

6 skin-on, bone-in chicken breast halves

3 tablespoons olive oil

1 pint fresh figs (about 12), halved lengthwise

2 shallots, thinly sliced

6 cloves fresh garlic, sliced

1 unpeeled lemon, sliced (about 9 slices)

1 cup port wine

¼ cup fresh flat-leaf parsley leaves for garnishing

Preheat an oven to 375°F. In a small bowl, mix the spices and salt. Lay the chicken on a baking sheet, piece of waxed paper, or plastic wrap and sprinkle each piece liberally on both sides with the spice mixture.

In a large nonstick skillet or sauté pan, heat the oil over medium-high heat until hot. Sauté half of the chicken for about 3 minutes on each side, or until the skin is deep golden brown and crispy. As the pieces are browned, place them, skin-side up, in a 9-by-13-inch roasting pan. Repeat with the remaining chicken.

Pour off any excess oil, then sauté the figs, shallots, garlic, and lemon for about 1 minute. Add the port and stir to scrape up the browned bits on the bottom of the pan. Bring just to a boil, and then add the hot mixture, with all the goodies, to the roasting pan, pouring it around, not over, the chicken to keep the browned crust intact.

Roast for about 40 to 45 minutes, or until the chicken is opaque throughout and nicely browned on the outside, with an internal temperature of 160°F.

Transfer the chicken to a platter or individual plates. Using a slotted spoon, retrieve the figs, shallots, garlic, and lemon slices from the sauce and distribute them over the chicken. Place the roasting pan on a burner on high heat and cook to reduce the sauce to about ¾ cup. Taste the sauce for seasoning, adjust if needed, then drizzle the sauce over the chicken and goodies. Scatter with parsley leaves for garnish.

CHEF'S NOTE: I suggest serving this dish with garlic mashed potatoes, a nice almond-studded rice pilaf, baked Delicata squash, or steamed green beans.

Punjabi Grilled Chicken Skewers with Spiced Herb Rub

MAKES 6 TO 8 SERVINGS

This spice rub illustrates the intersecting ethnic influences that help to define Northwest cuisine. Vancouver, British Columbia, benefits from a population of approximately sixty thousand East Indian immigrants. Its vibrant shopping district, Little India, is fragrant with exotic spices and authentic foods.

Rub

6 tablespoons olive oil

3 tablespoons finely chopped white onion

2 teaspoons minced fresh garlic

2 teaspoons cumin seed

2 teaspoons black mustard seed

2 tablespoons fresh lime juice

1 to 2 teaspoons minced, seeded jalapeño chile

¼ cup coarsely chopped fresh parsley

2 tablespoons coarsely chopped fresh mint

¼ cup coarsely chopped fresh cilantro

1 teaspoon salt

¼ teaspoon black pepper

1 tablespoon water

2 pounds boneless, skinless chicken thighs, cut into 1-inch chunks

Garnishes

Sour cream, thinned with a little water for drizzling, or yogurt

Fresh cilantro sprigs

To make the rub, heat 3 tablespoons of the oil in a nonstick skillet over medium heat. Cook the onion, uncovered, stirring occasionally, for 4 to 5 minutes, or until deep brown. Do not let the onion scorch. Add the garlic, cumin seed, and mustard seed and sauté for 30 seconds. Do not brown the garlic.

Remove from the heat and mix in the lime juice, jalapeño, fresh herbs, salt, and pepper. Transfer the mixture to a food processor and, with the machine running, drizzle in the remaining 3 tablespoons oil and the water and process to a paste-like consistency.

Toss the chicken pieces with the rub mixture and marinate, refrigerated, for at least 2 hours or preferably overnight.

Soak six to eight 10-inch bamboo skewers in water for at least 1 hour. Prepare a medium-hot fire in a charcoal grill, or preheat a gas grill to medium-high.

Thread the chicken on skewers and grill for about 5 to 6 minutes per side, or until opaque throughout.

To serve, drizzle with the thinned sour cream and garnish with cilantro sprigs.

CHEF'S NOTE: Accompany with basmati rice, grilled zucchini, and a chutney made with Northwest fruit, such as my Sour Cherry Ginger Chutney (see Sources, page 222). The rub would be excellent on fish or lamb, also.

Grilled Chicken with Fresh Corn Salsa

MAKES 6 SERVINGS

Brining has become very popular. While no longer a home preservation method, it's very trendy as a procedure for flavoring food and keeping meats moist. People are definitely trying this cooking practice with a vengeance, and I have incorporated it in this recipe along with the added zippiness of smoky chipotle chiles. If you don't have time for brining the chicken, you can always just lightly season it with salt and pepper and grill away.

Brine

4 cups water

2 tablespoons kosher salt

2 tablespoons packed brown sugar

2 teaspoons chipotle chile powder

1 tablespoon ground coriander

3 tablespoons minced fresh garlic

6 boneless, skinless chicken breast halves

Fresh Corn Salsa (recipe follows)

Garnishes

Lime wedges

Fresh cilantro sprigs

To make the brine, combine the ingredients in a large saucepan and bring to a simmer. Stir until the salt and sugar are dissolved, then remove from the heat and refrigerate for at least 2 hours, or until chilled. Submerge the chicken in the brine and refrigerate overnight, or for up to 12 hours.

Prepare a medium-hot fire in a charcoal grill, or preheat a gas grill to medium-high. While the grill is heating, prepare the salsa.

Drain the chicken well, then pat dry thoroughly. (Do not salt.) Discard the brine. Lightly oil the grill. Grill the chicken until nicely marked and opaque throughout but still moist, about 5 to 8 minutes per side, depending on your heat and the thickness of the chicken.

Serve the chicken on a platter or individual plates, spoon the salsa over the chicken, and garnish with lime wedges and cilantro sprigs. Diners squeeze the lime over the chicken and salsa.

Fresh Corn Salsa

MAKES 1½ CUPS

2 strips raw bacon, minced

½ cup ¼-inch-diced red bell pepper

½ cup ¼-inch-diced red onion

1 teaspoon minced fresh garlic

1 cup fresh or thawed frozen corn kernels

2 tablespoons fresh lime juice

1½ tablespoons packed brown sugar

⅛ teaspoon cayenne pepper

¼ to ½ teaspoon salt

2 tablespoons chopped fresh cilantro

In a 10-inch nonstick skillet over medium-high heat, cook the bacon until crisp, about 2 minutes. Add the bell pepper, onion, and garlic to the pan and sauté for 2 minutes, or until the mixture is just beginning to become soft.

Add the corn and sauté for 1 to 2 minutes more, then stir in the lime juice, brown sugar, cayenne, and salt and remove from the heat. Let cool, then stir in the cilantro. Serve at room temperature or slightly warm.

CHEF'S NOTE: You can make the salsa up to 1 day in advance, but wait until serving to add the cilantro.

Grilled Lamb Burgers on Warm Pitas with Yogurt Raita & Peppers

MAKES 4 SANDWICHES

Lamb burgers are in vogue on Northwest brewpub and casual café menus. The use of lamb in the region's cuisine stems not only from the culinary traditions of English and Scots colonists but also from those of the Basque sheepherders who came during the late nineteenth century and the East Indians who have settled in British Columbia. This recipe also uses peppers, of which hundreds of varieties—from super-spicy habaneros to long, sexy goat horns to orange-fleshed sweet bells—are grown in the hot regions of eastern Washington and Oregon. You could use whatever sizzles your palate.

Raita

½ cucumber, peeled, seeded, and coarsely grated
½ cup plain yogurt
¼ teaspoon dried dill weed
¾ teaspoon minced fresh garlic
1 teaspoon fresh lemon juice

Burgers

1½ pounds ground lamb
¾ teaspoon ground coriander
1 tablespoon minced fresh garlic
2 tablespoons minced onion
1½ teaspoons chopped fresh mint
1½ teaspoons chopped fresh oregano
1 teaspoon salt
½ teaspoon black pepper

4 large pita breads
1 bunch arugula, washed, spun dry, and torn into large pieces
½ cup thinly sliced roasted red bell peppers (see page 30)
1 teaspoon fresh lemon juice
1 teaspoon extra-virgin olive oil
Salt
Freshly ground black pepper

Prepare a medium-hot fire in a charcoal grill, or preheat a gas grill to medium-high.

To make the raita, squeeze the grated cucumber thoroughly to remove as much liquid as possible. Stir the cucumber and all the remaining raita ingredients in a small bowl.

To make the burgers, combine all the ingredients in a large bowl and, using clean hands, work the mixture until well combined. Divide the meat into 4 balls, then shape each into a 5- to 6-inch oval patty.

Grill the patties for about 3 to 5 minutes on each side, or until just cooked to your preferred doneness. Meanwhile, also grill the pita on each side until warmed, about 30 seconds per side.

In a small bowl, toss the arugula, peppers, lemon juice, and oil. Season with salt and pepper.

Cut each pita in half, straight down through both surfaces. Place a lamb patty on one half of each pita. Drizzle with a little raita and top with some of the arugula mixture. Close the sandwiches with the other halves of the pitas. Pass extra raita for dipping.

CHEF'S NOTE: The lamb patties can also be pan-fried over medium-high heat for about 3 to 5 minutes on each side, and the pita warmed in an oven.

Shepherd's Pie with Chèvre & Chive Mashed Potatoes

MAKES 6 TO 8 SERVINGS

The British will put almost anything in a pie. To "pie" actually means to jumble together, and shepherd's pie is just that. The dish is believed to have been developed in Scotland or northern England and was probably brought to the Pacific Northwest by settlers in British Columbia and Oregon. A mixture of leftover cooked lamb or beef, gravy, and vegetables, placed in a casserole or deep pie dish, is topped with whipped potatoes and baked until golden. My version has the addition of red wine and fresh rosemary, and the potato topping is enhanced with creamy chèvre stirred in.

Chèvre & Chive Mashed Potatoes
   (facing page)

1 tablespoon olive oil

1 large onion, chopped (about 2½ cups)

4 large carrots, diced (about 2½ cups)

1 large turnip, diced (about 2 cups)

1 leek, white part only, sliced, rinsed well,
   and diced (about ¾ cup)

1 pound ground lamb

1 pound ground beef

1 tablespoon minced fresh rosemary

½ cup dry red wine

3 tablespoons tomato paste

1 teaspoon salt

¼ teaspoon black pepper

3 tablespoons cornstarch

3 cups lamb, beef, or chicken stock or
   low-sodium beef broth

First, prepare the Chèvre & Chive Mashed Potatoes, and set aside. Preheat an oven to 400°F.

Heat the oil in a large skillet over medium-high heat and sauté the onion, carrots, turnip, and leek for about 4 to 6 minutes, or until tender. Remove with a slotted spoon and set aside.

To the same pan, add the meats and break up with a spoon. Cook the meat for about 5 minutes, or until browned. Carefully drain off any excess fat and return the pan to the heat. Stir in the rosemary, wine, tomato paste, salt, and pepper and scrape up the browned bits on the bottom of the pan as you bring the mixture to a boil.

Meanwhile, whisk the cornstarch into the stock and stir this mixture into the boiling meat mixture. Stirring constantly, cook for about 1 minute to thicken. Taste and adjust the seasoning as needed.

Transfer the mixture to a 9-by-13-inch baking dish. Spoon the mashed potatoes on top, covering the meat mixture evenly and making the top peaky-pretty. Bake for about 25 to 30 minutes, or until the mixture is bubbling and the top is lightly golden.

Chèvre & Chive Mashed Potatoes

2½ pounds unpeeled medium red potatoes, washed well and halved

Salt

1 cup milk or half-and-half

3 tablespoons butter

¼ teaspoon white pepper

4 ounces fresh goat cheese (chèvre), crumbled or cut into about 8 pieces

2 tablespoons thinly sliced fresh chives or very thinly sliced green onion tops

Put the potatoes in a very large pot and cover with water by at least 3 inches. Add a big pinch of salt. Bring to a boil, then reduce the heat and cook on a low boil until fork-tender, about 20 to 30 minutes. Test the potatoes to be sure they're tender all the way through.

Meanwhile, heat the milk and butter in a small saucepan over low heat until the butter is melted and the milk is warm. Do not boil. Keep warm.

When the potatoes are cooked, quickly drain them well in a large colander, then return them to the pot. Shake the pot over low heat for about 30 seconds to dry out any remaining water. Remove from the heat and add the milk mixture. (Both the potatoes and the liquid must be hot.) With a heavy-duty whisk or masher, mash the potatoes. Then add 1 teaspoon of salt, the white pepper, and cheese, and whip or mash the potatoes until they are fluffy. Mix in the chives and cover the potatoes to keep warm.

VEGGIES AND SIDES

Colorful Scallion **Fried Rice**

MAKES 6 TO 8 SERVINGS

Thanks to the large Chinese population in the Northwest, I have been eating fried rice since I was too young to remember. It is still one of my favorite things when done well. My version is more pan-Asian fusion than strictly Chinese; these days you see a lot of this type of variation in restaurants from Vancouver, B.C., to Portland.

Rice

2 cups jasmine rice

1 teaspoon salt

3 cups water

1 fresh or frozen Kaffir lime leaf (optional)

3 eggs

1/4 teaspoon salt

1 tablespoon water

4 tablespoons vegetable oil

1 cup thinly sliced shiitake mushrooms
   (about 5 ounces)

2 teaspoons minced peeled fresh ginger

1/4 cup 1/4-inch-diced carrots

1 tablespoon minced fresh garlic

2 tablespoons minced fresh lemongrass,
   white part only (optional)

1/4 cup 1/4-inch-diced red bell pepper

3/4 cup thinly sliced green onion

2 tablespoons soy sauce

Cook the rice the day before, or at least 2 hours in advance, and refrigerate. First, rinse the rice in a strainer until the water runs clear. Shake the rice and drain well.

To cook the rice in a rice cooker, combine the drained rice in the cooker with the 1 teaspoon salt, 3 cups water, and lime leaf (if using). Stir well, cover, and steam until tender, per the manufacturer's instructions.

To cook the rice without a rice cooker, preheat an oven to 400°F. Combine the drained rice in a large ovenproof saucepan with the 1 teaspoon salt, 3 cups water, and lime leaf (if using). Bring to a boil over high heat and stir. Quickly cover the pan with a piece of foil and a tight-fitting lid. Transfer the pan to the oven and cook for 15 to 20 minutes, or until rice is tender. When the rice is cooked, immediately remove the lid and foil.

Fluff the cooked rice very well with a fork, making sure the grains are separated. Let cool, then refrigerate.

When ready to finish the dish, have all remaining ingredients prepared and within reach of the range.

In a small bowl, whisk the eggs with the salt and water. Heat 1 tablespoon of the oil in a wok or large (at least 12-inch-diameter), heavy nonstick skillet or sauté pan over medium-high heat. Add the eggs and, with a spatula, lift the eggs as they cook, letting the uncooked part run underneath until set. Transfer the cooked eggs to a cutting board and let cool while you fry the rice, then cut the eggs into 1/4-inch-wide strips.

Accompaniments

Soy sauce

Sambal oelek or Asian chili condiment

Lime wedges

Fresh cilantro sprigs

To fry the rice, heat 1 tablespoon of the oil in the same wok or pan over medium-high heat. Stir-fry the mushrooms until soft, about 45 seconds to 1 minute. Add the remaining 2 tablespoons oil and heat. Add the ginger, carrot, garlic, lemongrass (if using), and cooked rice. Let sit a minute or so, then stir-fry for about 1 minute. Repeat, letting the rice sit a bit before each stir-frying, so that the rice gets some nice golden color on it. The total stir-frying should take about 4 to 5 minutes. Add the bell pepper, green onion, and cooked eggs. Stir-fry for about 1 minute more, or until heated through, then drizzle with the 2 tablespoons soy sauce and toss well.

Serve immediately and pass the soy sauce, sambal oelek, lime wedges, and cilantro separately for guests to "customize" and season their rice the way they like it.

CHEF'S NOTE: To achieve that genuine "fried rice" consistency, cook and refrigerate the rice the day before, then let it sit at room temperature for 30 minutes before frying. Or, use 6 cups leftover "take-out" rice, but be sure to season it a bit more with salt and soy.

Sesame Snap Peas

MAKES 4 TO 6 SERVINGS

Sugar snap peas come into the farmers' markets in late May and early June. The spring-happy shoppers can't even wait to get them home to cook—but start crunching these sweet pods as they shop. At Asian markets, such as the fabulous Chinatown fresh markets in Vancouver and Richmond, British Columbia, or Washington and Oregon's Japanese grocery heaven, Uwajimaya, you'll find not only snap peas but a plethora of "choys" as well. (Any of those greens would also work well in this recipe.)

Glaze

½ cup soy sauce

¼ cup dry sherry wine

4 teaspoons packed brown sugar

1 tablespoon minced peeled fresh ginger

1 tablespoon minced fresh garlic

¼ teaspoon red pepper flakes

1 tablespoon cornstarch

1 tablespoon Asian sesame oil

2 cups thinly sliced, stemmed shiitake
  mushrooms (about 10 ounces)

1½ pounds (8 cups) sugar snap pea pods
  or snow peas

¼ cup sesame seed, toasted (see page 30),
  for garnishing

To make the glaze, whisk the glaze ingredients in a small bowl and set aside.

In a large nonstick skillet or sauté pan, heat the sesame oil over high heat, and sauté the mushrooms, stirring, for about 2 minutes, or until soft. Immediately add the pea pods and, working quickly, rewhisk the glaze, then add it to the pan. Cover tightly with a lid and cook for 1 to 2 minutes, or until the pea pods are just crisp-tender and brilliant green. Remove the lid and stir the peas, making sure the glaze is reduced and coating the pea pods nicely. Sprinkle with sesame seed for garnish.

CHEF'S NOTE: You can make these 1 day in advance if desired. The dish can be served hot, chilled, or at room temperature. If you are making it ahead and chilling, spread the cooked pea pods out on a baking sheet to cool before refrigerating.

Zucchini Fritter-Cakes with Spicy Fresh Tomato Sauce

MAKES 8 CAKES, OR ABOUT 4 SERVINGS

Summertime garden zucchini are prolific. I've heard stories of people going on outings in the wee hours for sneak-a-zucchini-onto-your-neighbor's-porch night. There are all-zucchini luncheons and zucchini festivals. The historic Washington town of Oakville holds a Zucchini Jubilee in September; there are contests for zucchini decorating and carving, a cook-off, and zuke-rod races.

Sauce

2 tablespoons olive oil

2 ripe tomatoes, diced (1 cup)

2 teaspoons minced fresh garlic

1 tablespoon minced jalapeño chile

2 tablespoons finely chopped fresh cilantro

¼ teaspoon salt

2 teaspoons minced fresh garlic

1 egg

6 tablespoons flour

¼ teaspoon baking powder

¾ teaspoon salt

⅛ teaspoon cayenne pepper

1 tablespoon sour cream

6 tablespoons grated hard Northwest cheese, such as Quillisascut manchego, or grated Parmesan cheese

2 cups coarsely grated zucchini

Vegetable oil for frying

Garnishes

Sour cream

Fresh cilantro sprigs

Lime wedges for squeezing

To make the sauce, heat the oil in a nonstick skillet over medium-high heat. Sauté the tomatoes for about 1 minute, stir in the garlic and jalapeño, and sauté for about 30 seconds more. Remove from the heat and stir in the cilantro and salt. Cover and set aside while you make the fritter-cakes.

Whisk the garlic, egg, flour, baking powder, salt, and cayenne in a medium bowl. Stir in the sour cream and cheese.

With clean hands, squeeze the zucchini well to remove extra moisture. (This is an important step!) Stir the zucchini into the batter.

Heat a large nonstick skillet over medium to medium-high heat and coat the skillet with about 2 teaspoons oil (as you would for cooking pancakes). Cooking the fritter-cakes in batches and adjusting the heat as you go, drop the batter by ⅛ cupfuls (2 tablespoons). Cook the fritters for about 1½ to 2 minutes on each side, or until golden brown and cooked through. As the fritters are done, transfer them to a baking sheet lined with paper towels and keep warm.

Serve the fritter-cakes topped with the warm sauce; dollop with a little sour cream and garnish with cilantro sprigs and lime wedges.

CHEF'S NOTE: Whisk up the batter just before cooking the fritter-cakes; do not make it in advance. (If made ahead, the zucchini will purge moisture and the batter will become too wet.) These fritters make a satisfying breakfast entrée when topped with a poached egg, and if you make tiny fritter-cakes, you can serve them as a passed appetizer.

WILD VEGGIES AND SUCH: OREGON TRUFFLES, SEA BEANS, CATTAILS, FIDDLEHEADS, AND STINGING NETTLES

Wild and delectable things grow in the Northwest, ready for gathering by the skilled and persistent seeker.

In Oregon, winter black truffles show up sporadically at farmers' markets and high-end grocers between November and March. The spring white Oregon truffle was declared by James Beard, the late Oregon-born culinary legend, to be at least equal to the Italian white truffle in taste. These truffles grow at the base of Douglas fir trees and are found on the west side of the Cascades all the way up into southern British Columbia.

Then, of course, there are the wild vegetables lauded so lavishly by gourmet foragers. From the salty crisp sea beans and edible seaweeds that grace some of our saltwater shores to the stinging nettles growing at forest margins, these prizes are in demand by spring gourmands.

Tender young cattail shoots can be steamed like asparagus. The rhizomes can also be eaten or dried and ground for flour.

For several weeks in late spring or into early summer, sea beans, or sea asparagus if you're in Canada, are found in brackish river estuaries all along our coast. Sea beans are used fresh as a crunchy garnish, blanched for salads, battered and fried in tempura, and pickled for year-round fun. They're a kicky garnish for a Caesar cocktail, a Canadian Bloody Mary made with clamato juice!

Fiddleheads are another early-spring wild food. Named for the tightly curled young shoot of the ostrich fern before it unfurls, fiddleheads are especially sought after in British Columbia and southern Alaska. The shoots are usually sautéed, steamed, stir-fried, blanched and marinated, or pickled.

And in spite of the prickly plant's sting, nettles are gathered as a palatable and nutritious food. Found along country roadsides, trails, stream banks, and at the edges of woods, they are best picked in early spring when the most desirable young leaves and shoots appear before flowering. Nettles are most commonly cooked like spinach and are also favored in delicate-tasting spring soups; the cooking process eliminates the sting.

Walla Walla "French Onion" Mashed Potatoes

Two famed Washington ingredients give a fun play on a retro flavor profile: the creamy, naturally pale yellow flesh of Yukon Gold potatoes is mashed up with sherried, caramelized Walla Walla Sweet onions. Yum! Bring it on with a piece of grilled salmon and a glass of seductive Oregon pinot noir.

2 pounds (about 6 medium) Yukon Gold potatoes, whole or halved, depending on size

Salt

6 tablespoons butter

2 cups chopped Walla Walla Sweet onions

¼ cup dry sherry (optional)

½ cup milk or half-and-half

¼ teaspoon white pepper

¾ cup (3 ounces) shredded Gruyère cheese

Minced fresh chives or parsley for garnishing

Put the potatoes in a very large pot and cover with water by at least 3 inches. Add a pinch of salt. Bring to a boil, then reduce the heat and cook the potatoes on a low boil until fork-tender, about 20 to 30 minutes. Test the potatoes to be sure they're tender all the way through.

Meanwhile, in a large nonstick skillet or sauté pan, melt 2 tablespoons of the butter over medium heat. Sauté the onions for about 10 to 15 minutes, or until caramelized to a golden brown. Add the sherry (if using) and sauté for about 30 seconds to 1 minute more, or until the liquid has evaporated. Remove from the heat.

While the potatoes are cooking, combine the milk, white pepper, ¾ teaspoon salt, and the remaining 4 tablespoons butter in a small saucepan. Heat over low heat until the butter is melted and the milk is warm; do not boil. Keep warm.

When the potatoes are done, drain them well in a large colander, then return them to the pot. Shake the pot over low heat for about 30 seconds to dry out any remaining water. Remove from the heat and add half of the hot liquid mixture. (Both the potatoes and the liquid must be hot.) With a heavy-duty whisk or masher, mash the potatoes. Add the remaining liquid and whip or mash the potatoes until fluffy.

Fold in the caramelized onions and shredded cheese. Mound the potatoes in a warm large bowl. Sprinkle with chives or parsley.

Savory Chanterelle **Bread Pudding**

MAKES 6 TO 8 SERVINGS

You know it's fall in the Northwest when the air gets damp and the rains start to come, mixed in with a few days of sunshine. We wild-mushroom foragers hit the trails to scope out our cherished spots, and fungi enthusiasts get all excited as the coveted chanterelles begin to pop up in the moist ground. This unique bread pudding is wonderful served with Herb-Lacquered Chicken with Red Wine Cranberry Compote (page 150). Or try it instead of traditional stuffing alongside your holiday turkey.

1 tablespoon olive oil or butter

2 cups cleaned and sliced chanterelles
(about 10 ounces)

1/2 cup diced onion

1/3 cup diced celery

1 tablespoon minced fresh garlic

4 cups 1-inch-cubed firm, rustic French- or
Italian-style bread

1 1/2 tablespoons minced fresh sage

1 tablespoon minced fresh thyme or lemon
thyme

1 1/2 teaspoons salt

1/4 teaspoon black pepper

1 1/2 cups half-and-half

1 1/2 cups milk

2 eggs

2 egg yolks

Preheat an oven to 325°F. Heat the oil in a large sauté pan or skillet over medium-high heat. Sauté the chanterelles and onion for 3 to 4 minutes, or until three-quarters done. Add the celery and sauté for about 1 1/2 to 2 minutes more. Add the garlic and sauté for 30 seconds more, taking care not to burn the garlic. Remove from the heat.

Combine the bread cubes, herbs, salt, and pepper in a large bowl. Mix in the cooked mushroom mixture and set aside.

Butter a 6-cup glass or ceramic baking dish or spray with vegetable-oil cooking spray.

Whisk the half-and-half, milk, eggs, and egg yolks in a medium bowl. Pour the egg mixture into the bread mixture and mix gently and thoroughly. Transfer the mixture to the baking dish and level out the surface, lightly pressing the bread down into the dish.

Bake for 50 to 60 minutes, or until the custard is just set in the center. Do not overbake or the custard will scramble.

CHEF'S NOTE: It is important to use a rustic-style bread for this recipe—not airy bread.

Rosemary Roasted Squash

MAKES ABOUT 6 SERVINGS

Danish, golden and white acorns, Sweet Mamas, butternuts, Hubbards, Sweet Dumplings—in the late summer and fall the farmers' market tables overflow with mountains of multihued hard-shelled winter squash. When shopping for this recipe, any of these will do fine, but try to find organic squash as they tend to be more flavorful. And if you get a monster squash and can't figure out how to "get it open," do as I do: head out to the backyard and throw it as hard as you can on the ground. That usually does the trick!

2 tablespoons olive oil

2 tablespoons packed brown sugar

2 tablespoons fresh lemon juice

1 tablespoon minced fresh rosemary

1½ teaspoons kosher salt

½ teaspoon black pepper

8 cups peeled 1½-inch-cubed winter squash, such as Hubbard, butternut, or acorn

Fresh rosemary sprigs for garnishing (optional)

Preheat an oven to 375°F. In a large bowl, whisk the oil, brown sugar, lemon juice, rosemary, salt, and pepper. Add the squash and toss to coat well with the mixture.

Lightly oil a rimmed baking sheet or spray with vegetable-oil cooking spray. Lay the squash in a single layer on the pan. Use two pans if necessary; do not crowd the squash. Roast the squash for about 20 to 25 minutes, or until it is tender and some edges are caramelized.

If serving on a platter, garnish with sprigs of rosemary, if desired.

CHEF'S NOTE: Purchase about 4 to 5 pounds of whole squash to make 8 cups of diced squash.

Whipped Cauliflower Gratin with Dijon Mustard

MAKES 6 TO 8 SERVINGS

Mustard is a lively taste-enhancer. Dijon—once viewed by Americans as the exclusive province of chefs, food snobs, and gourmets—has become a staple in the American kitchen. It's a "must" in many of my recipes. I often use Dijon, as in this dish, to add a "layer" of tanginess and round out the flavor profile.

1 large head cauliflower

1/3 cup heavy whipping cream

1/4 cup sour cream

3 tablespoons butter

1 tablespoon Dijon mustard

1/2 teaspoon salt

1/4 teaspoon white pepper

3/4 cup (3 ounces) shredded Gruyère cheese

2 tablespoons thinly sliced fresh chives
   for garnishing

Preheat an oven to 350°F. Lightly spray a 6-cup gratin dish with vegetable-oil cooking spray or brush with olive oil.

Break the cauliflower into florets (you should have about 6 cups) and cook in a large pot of salted boiling water until totally tender, about 5 minutes. (The florets should be "mashable" but not mushy.)

Drain well, then process in a food processor with the heavy cream, sour cream, butter, mustard, salt, and pepper until the mixture is a smooth, thick purée. Pulse in 1/2 cup of the cheese.

Transfer the mixture to the baking dish and sprinkle with the remaining cheese. Bake for 30 to 35 minutes, or until heated through and the cheese is melted and slightly browned. Sprinkle with chives to garnish.

CHEF'S NOTE: This is a nice low-carb dish.

FARMERS' MARKETS, GIANT VEGETABLES, P-PATCHES, AND CELEBRITY COMPOSTING

The Pike Place Market is the very heartbeat of Seattle; it was established in 1907 and has been bringing the farmers directly to the residents ever since. The oldest continuously operated market in the U.S., it abounds with honeys, dairy products, meats, and fish. The resurgence of farmers' markets began in the 1970s; the Granville Island Farmers' Truck Market pioneered the trend in Vancouver, B.C.'s reclaimed former industrial zone. And the straight-to-the-consumer phenomenon continues unabated; there are now more than 250 farmers' markets, from Delta Junction, Alaska, to Ashland, Oregon.

Shoppers clamber for heirloom tomatoes, fava beans, organic fingerling potatoes, old-fashioned apple varieties, and picked-this-morning corn. Local farmers have brought new diversity to our tables and influenced our eating habits. Urbanites now routinely dine on Asian greens, such as edible pea vines, baby bok choy, and gai lan (Chinese broccoli), as well as frisée, rainbow chard, and garlic shoots. In addition to farm-fresh veggies, many of the markets offer organic meats, breads, and pastries, plus cottage-industry jams, pickles, and preserves. In some areas, seafood, wild-picked berries and mushrooms, and wines direct from the producer are also available.

You might be surprised that Alaska, "land of the midnight sun," is part of this movement, but there are approximately a million acres of agricultural land being farmed in that state. Commercial vegetable production is primarily in the Matanuska Valley around Palmer, located forty-five miles northeast of Anchorage. From June through August, there is twenty-hour daylight and then a four-hour period of twilight. So, while the growing season is short, the extended day length partially makes up for it, and the area is famous for raising gigantic produce and flowers. Whopper-size fruits and vegetables are exhibited at the state fair. Record holders include a 32-pound table beet, a 13-pound white radish, and a 168-pound watermelon. More "standard" entries include cabbages ranging from 50 to 70 pounds, 12-pound carrots, and 30-pound bunches of celery. Alaskans need to be sure to adjust recipes calling for one stalk of celery!

Way farther south, there is a different kind of gardening going on. In Seattle, the Department of Neighborhoods coordinates the P-Patch program in conjunction with the nonprofit Friends of P-Patch to provide community organic garden space for city residents. Some 1,900 plots serve more than 4,600 gardeners on 12 acres of land spread out among 54 P-Patches. Special programs serve low-income, disabled, youth, and non-English-speaking populations. The Interbay P-Patch has attracted quite a bit of attention for its Celebrity Composting program. Local glitterati are invited to the garden on Saturdays for the "compost social." The dignitaries and notables turn a bin of compost—and in turn they get the compost bin named after them. Afterward everyone gathers round for some homemade soup and bread. P-Patch gardeners supply seven to ten tons of fresh organic vegetables to area food banks each year.

WELCOME TO YOUR NEIGHBORHOOD P-PATCH COMMUNITY GARDEN

- Please come in and enjoy this organic garden sanctuary
- Your neighbors lovingly care for the spaces in this garden
- The produce and flowers grown here belong to the gardeners
- Please don't pick anything or disturb the garden
- If you want to garden here or in any other community garden in Seattle, call #684-0264

This organic community garden is made possible through the following partnerships: Neighborhood volunteers, Friends of P-Patch, Department of Neighborhoods P-Patch Program

Persons pilfering, damaging plants, dumping material, or destroying property are subject to arrest under ordinance #102843.

City of Seattle Department of Neighborhoods

SEATTLE P-PATCH

Friends of P-Patch

West Seattle community P-Patch

Green & Yellow Pole Beans Provençal

My Grandmother Mimi used to make a sweet mustard sauce to go over steamed green beans, which I have always loved. I've come back to that trusty mustard-with-beans combination here. This colorful dish can also be served at room temperature, so it's a splendid veggie to bring along to a potluck dinner party or outdoor soirée.

¼ cup extra-virgin olive oil

1 small Walla Walla Sweet onion, thinly sliced

1 pound green beans, trimmed and halved crosswise (about 4 cups)

1 pound wax beans, trimmed and halved crosswise (about 4 cups)

¼ cup dry white wine

1 pint cherry tomatoes, halved

1 tablespoon minced fresh garlic

2 tablespoons red wine vinegar

2 tablespoons whole-grain mustard

1 tablespoon minced fresh thyme

½ cup pitted kalamata olives, coarsely chopped

1 teaspoon kosher salt

¼ teaspoon freshly ground black pepper

In a large nonstick skillet or sauté pan over medium-high heat, heat the oil until fragrant. Sauté the onion, stirring often, for about 4 minutes, or until golden. Transfer the onion to a large bowl.

Add the green and wax beans and white wine to the pan, cover, and steam the beans just until their color is bright, about 2 minutes. Remove the lid, add the tomatoes and garlic, and sauté until the beans are just crisp-tender, about 1 to 2 minutes more.

Meanwhile, to the onion in the bowl, add the vinegar, mustard, thyme, and olives, then toss in the beans as soon as they are done. Toss in the salt and pepper; taste and adjust the seasoning as desired.

Dungeness Crab & Artichoke Stuffed Potatoes

MAKES 4 SERVINGS

Artichoke-and-crab dip is a Northwest party favorite. So, hey! let's make a meal of it. Washington russets are an ideal foil to the rich stuffing—and a little jalapeño adds just the right kick! Use smaller potatoes to serve these as a fantastic side dish to a big juicy steak. Or select big ones to present it as an entrée in itself— just pair with a crunchy salad and a glass of Northwest chardonnay.

4 unpeeled large Washington russet
  potatoes, scrubbed

1 small package (3 ounces) cream cheese

1/4 cup milk

1/4 cup mayonnaise

1/3 cup thinly sliced green onions

1 tablespoon minced pickled jalapeño chile
  (less if you don't like it spicy)

2 teaspoons minced fresh garlic

3/4 cup (3 ounces) shredded Parmesan cheese,
  plus more for sprinkling

1 pound Dungeness crabmeat

1 can (13 to 14 ounces) artichoke heart
  quarters, drained well and coarsely
  chopped

Preheat an oven to 400°F. Prick the potatoes and bake for 45 to 55 minutes, or until very tender and baked through. Remove from the oven and let sit for 10 minutes. (Leave the oven on.)

Meanwhile, combine the cream cheese, milk, mayonnaise, green onions, jalapeño, and garlic in a mixing bowl. Using an electric mixer fitted with a whisk attachment, mix until combined.

After the potatoes have cooled for 10 minutes, cut the tops off (lengthwise) and scoop out the hot potato with a spoon, leaving a 1/2-inch shell. Add the potato pulp to the mixing bowl and mix with the whisk attachment until well mixed. Stir in the 3/4 cup cheese, the crabmeat, and artichokes.

Scoop the mixture back into the potato shells, dividing it evenly and piling up. Sprinkle with extra cheese for pretty tops. Put the potatoes on a baking sheet and bake for about 20 to 25 minutes, or until golden and heated through.

CHEF'S NOTE: If you want to make these in advance, bring them to room temperature for 45 minutes before the final baking.

Mediterranean Potato Salad

MAKES 6 TO 8 SERVINGS

Everyone loves old-fashioned picnicky, or what I call dish-up, salads. Look at potato salad—how many versions can there be? Sweet German; mustardy-eggy Mom's-style; hip sweet potato with spicy chutney dressing. This recipe's lightened up with lots of veggies—all tossed with an oregano-and-feta vinaigrette. I love this served with simply prepared chicken, fish, or shrimp.

2 pounds red potatoes, cut into 1-inch pieces
   (about 6 cups)
2 tablespoons red wine vinegar
¼ cup extra-virgin olive oil
1 tablespoon Dijon mustard
1 tablespoon chopped fresh oregano
2 tablespoons chopped fresh mint (optional)
½ teaspoon salt
¼ teaspoon black pepper
½ cup halved, pitted kalamata olives
1 cucumber, peeled, seeded, and diced
½ cup chopped roasted red peppers
   (see page 30)
1 small green bell pepper, diced
½ cup tiny-diced red onion
1 cup (4 ounces) crumbled feta cheese
¼ cup chopped fresh flat-leaf parsley

Steam the potatoes in a steamer or over boiling water in a covered pot for 10 to 14 minutes, or until very tender.

Meanwhile, in a large bowl, whisk the vinegar, oil, mustard, oregano, mint (if using), salt, and pepper. While the potatoes are still warm, toss them with the dressing.

Set aside until cool, then stir in the remaining ingredients.

"Green" Rice Prima Vera with Asparagus, Peas & Pods

MAKES 6 SERVINGS

This preparation is a beautiful study in texture and shades of green—d'lish with Grilled Salmon with Herbed Walla Walla Sweet Onions (page 112). And if you live near an Asian market or are a gardener yourself, garnish the dish with edible pea vines—lightly sautéed or just in their fresh state.

1 cup basmati rice, rinsed and drained well

1½ cups water

½ cup chopped fresh parsley

3 tablespoons butter

¾ cup ¼-inch-diced onion

1½ teaspoons minced fresh garlic

1½ teaspoons minced lemon zest

1 tablespoon fresh lemon juice

2 tablespoons heavy whipping cream

1¼ teaspoons salt

Vegetables

1 tablespoon olive oil

¾ cup snap or snow pea pods, trimmed, stringed, and cut into diagonal slices

¾ cup diagonally sliced asparagus

½ cup fresh or partially defrosted frozen green peas

Salt

Freshly ground black pepper

2 tablespoons thinly sliced fresh chives

Garnish

Fresh pea vines

Preheat an oven to 375°F. Put the drained rice in a 6-cup baking dish.

Combine the water and parsley in a blender and blend to chop the parsley very fine.

Melt the butter in a medium nonstick or heavy saucepan over medium heat. Sauté the onion for about 2 minutes, or until soft. Add the garlic and cook for about 30 seconds; do not brown. Add the parsley mixture, being sure to scrape all the parsley into the pan. Add the lemon zest and juice, cream, and salt and bring to a boil.

Stir the mixture into the rice, being sure to scrape up and include all the goodies. Seal tightly with foil and bake for about 20 to 25 minutes, or until the rice is tender and all the liquid is absorbed. When the rice is done, fluff with a fork and keep warm while finishing the vegetables.

To cook the vegetables, during the last few minutes before the rice is done, heat the oil in a skillet or sauté pan over medium to medium-high heat. Sauté the pea pods and asparagus for about 1½ minutes. Add the shelled peas and sauté for about 30 seconds more, or until just tender. Season the vegetables to taste with salt and pepper, then fold the vegetables and chives into the rice. Garnish with pea vines.

ARTISANAL AND LOCAL CHEESE MAKERS

In the early 1980s, small-scale artisanal cheese started to become part of the Northwest foodie scene. Artisanal, or handcrafted, cheeses typically have much more individual character than commercially produced cheeses. The cheese maker attends to the cheeses individually, aging them according to his or her judgment rather than following a factory schedule. If a farmstead cheese is made from pasteurized milk, it has usually been pasteurized at a lower temperature than that used for commercial cheese, so the cheese doesn't taste "cooked."

Another source of variation in the cheese is from the diets the animals are fed. Subtle differences in the milk occur as the animals are usually rotated through a property's different pastures where a range of browse is available to them.

Washington state cheese pioneer Sally Jackson uses milk from her herd at her farm in Oroville near the Canadian border. Her products include both soft and hard goat's-milk cheeses, sheep's-milk cheeses, and semihard cow's-milk cheeses. They are often enhanced with jalapeño chile and garlic or dried tomatoes and oregano from her garden. Sally Jackson's cheeses caught the attention of Northwest chefs early in the American cheese renaissance, and today her cheeses are delivered to restaurants and retail cheese shops throughout the region.

At Quillisascut Cheese Company, in Rice, Washington, Lora Lea and Rick Misterly have been making cow's- and goat's-milk cheeses since 1987. Quillisascut's superb raw-milk aged manchego-style cheese is well known, as is their smooth and tangy chèvre.

Suzanne and Roger Wechsler, owners of Samish Bay Cheese since 1999, are relative newcomers in the arena. They produce organic farmstead cheeses from a mixed herd of Jersey, Milking Shorthorn, Dutch Belted, and cross-breeds, raising most of the cows' feed right on their Rootabaga Country Farm in Bow, Washington. Their Gouda, mild and creamy when young then sharper, drier, and more crumbly when aged, is available both plain and flavored with herbs, nettles, cumin, or caraway. And their Montasio is a full-flavored hard grating cheese in the tradition of the Friuli-Venezia Giulia region in northeastern Italy.

Two even newer Washington cheese producers are Beecher's Handmade Cheese, which is located right in the Pike Place Market, where you can watch the cheese being made, and the already-much-esteemed Estrella Family Creamery in Montesano, which has every local chef and connoisseur smacking his or her lips. Beecher's Flagship is a semihard nutty-flavored cheese aged for a full year, and their Tranquility is smooth and buttery; both are cow's-milk cheeses. Estrella milks about three dozen grass-fed animals—cows, goats, and a few sheep—and offers about ten raw-milk farmstead cheeses at any one time. Their Cheddar-style Black Creek Buttery is made from a blend of all three milks. The cow's-milk Wynoochee River Blue attracted attention almost immediately. Among their other cheeses are a havarti, a Camembert-style Mélange, and a washed-rind Tomme de Marc.

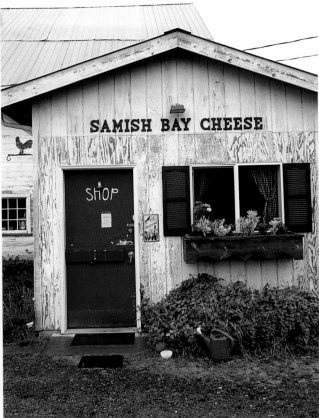

Pierre Kolisch, of Juniper Grove Farms in central Oregon's high-desert plateau, is a long-established farmstead cheese maker. He makes a dozen types of goat's-milk cheese and uses raw milk where legally permitted, which in the United States means the cheese must have been aged at least sixty days. His mold-ripened Pyramid, salty pecorino Redmondo, and ashed Dutchman's Flat are all raw-milk cheeses. The farm's signature cheese is its aged, washed-rind raw-milk Tumalo Tomme.

Larger commercial production comes from Oregon's Tillamook County Creamery Association, a century-old farmer-owned cooperative. Tillamook sharp Cheddar graces many a backyard-grilled burger and lunchtime sandwich. Also in Oregon is the Rogue Creamery, which produces an astonishing blue-vein Oregonzola and the award-winning Smokey Blue—their renowned Oregon Blue smoked overnight with hazelnut shells.

British Columbia also has a variety of artisanal cheese makers. Gort's Gouda in Salmon Arm makes Gouda, feta, and yogurt. David Wood's Salt Spring Island operation crafts an assortment of goat's-milk cheeses. The Carmelis dairy also makes 100 percent goat's-milk cheeses, from soft and tangy to hard aged pecorino.

But the most idiosyncratic Northwest cheese producer has to be the Washington State University Creamery, where cheese has been made and sold in a thirty-ounce can since 1940. This unusual packaging was developed to send cheese overseas. The creamery currently produces over 220,000 cans of cheese each year, 75 percent of which is Cougar Gold, their white Cheddar. It keeps indefinitely refrigerated; the longer it ages the sharper and drier it gets, until it resembles a fine Parmigiano-Reggiano. I have a can from 1989 that I am saving for a super-special cheesy occasion!

Just remember, with any fine cheese, to bring it to room temperature for about an hour or so before serving. This will release its full taste and aroma and let you experience the cheese at its best texture.

Super-Sexy Noodles with Artisanal Cheese & a Pouf of Herbs

MAKES 6 TO 8 SERVINGS AS AN ACCOMPANIMENT OR 4 TO 6 AS AN ENTRÉE

The artisanal cheese movement was slow to take off—but there is no stopping it now. In the early eighties, there were only a few cheese makers in the Northwest, one of them being the groundbreaking Sally Jackson, who did not even have a phone when I first started buying from her. She lived "way on the other side of the mountains" in the Okanogan Highlands and used to send a postcard when she was coming to Seattle. Now, there are more than thirty cheese makers in Alaska, British Columbia, Washington, and Oregon, so you should be able to find a winner! Try pairing these noodles with Sage-Roasted Pork Loin with Apples & Onions (page 138).

3 tablespoons butter

2½ teaspoons minced fresh garlic

3 tablespoons flour

1 cup heavy whipping cream

1½ cups milk

1¼ teaspoons kosher salt

Pinch of cayenne pepper

4 ounces local artisanal cheese of your liking, such as a combination of a double-cream and a slightly stinky cheese, crumbled

¼ cup tiny, picked leaves of fresh curly parsley

1 tablespoon fresh tarragon leaves, torn

1 tablespoon very thinly sliced fresh basil leaves

2 tablespoons ½-inch pieces fresh chives

1 pound dried gemelli pasta

1 cup (4 ounces) grated artisanal hard cheese or Parmesan cheese

Melt the butter in a medium saucepan over medium-high heat. Sauté the garlic for 15 seconds, but do not brown. Whisk in the flour and continue whisking for 15 seconds while bubbling and beginning to brown slightly. Vigorously whisk in the cream, milk, salt, and cayenne. Bring the sauce to a simmer, whisking occasionally, for 6 to 8 minutes, or until it thickens. Remove the sauce from the heat and stir in the softer cheeses to melt.

While the sauce is simmering, gently toss the parsley, tarragon, basil, and chives in a small bowl. Set aside.

Meanwhile, in a large pot of salted boiling water, cook the pasta per package instructions until al dente. Drain well and keep warm. When the sauce is done, mix the pasta, sauce, and three-fourths of the grated cheese in the pasta-cooking pot.

Divide the noodles among serving plates and sprinkle each with some of the remaining grated cheese. Top with a pouf of the herb mixture.

Blue Cheese Scalloped Potatoes

MAKES 12 SERVINGS

I created this recipe for the Washington State Potato Commission, and it has become their most popular recipe, so I just had to include it. Even non-blue-cheese-lovers love this dish, as it has just the right amount of blue cheese for a nice kick.

Potatoes

5 pounds russet potatoes

2 teaspoons salt

1/2 teaspoon black pepper

2 teaspoons minced fresh thyme

3/4 cup (3 ounces) crumbled blue cheese

3/4 cup (3 ounces) grated Parmesan cheese

Sauce

1 cup sour cream

2 cups heavy whipping cream

1 teaspoon salt

Garnish

Fresh thyme sprigs

Preheat an oven to 350°F. Butter a 9-by-13-inch baking dish.

To prepare the potatoes, peel and cut them into 1/8-inch-thick slices. Toss them in a large bowl with the salt, pepper, and thyme. In a small bowl, mix the cheeses.

Layer half the potatoes in the prepared baking dish. Sprinkle with half the cheese mixture, then layer with the remaining potatoes.

To make the sauce, whisk the ingredients in a bowl and pour the mixture over the potatoes. Tap the baking dish on the counter to spread the sauce and release any air bubbles. Sprinkle with the remaining cheese.

Bake for about 1 1/4 to 1 1/2 hours, or until browned and completely tender all the way through when poked in the center with a knife.

Garnish with thyme sprigs and serve immediately.

CHEF'S NOTES: You can also make this recipe in advance, then let cool and store, covered and refrigerated, for up to 2 days. Bring to room temperature and reheat, covered, in a preheated 350°F oven until hot.

Guests are very impressed when I serve these potatoes as individual round towers. Chill the cooked potatoes until totally cold (overnight is best). Cut them into 12 cylinders with a deep 2 1/2-inch-diameter cutter. (You can find these standard-size biscuit cutters at gourmet cooking shops.) Place the potato towers on a parchment-lined baking sheet. Poke a 4-inch bamboo skewer straight down through the center of each tower to hold it together and refrigerate, tented, until needed. Reheat them in a preheated 400°F oven until warmed through and nicely browned, about 6 to 10 minutes. Using a small spatula, transfer each tower (with the skewer still in place) to a serving plate, then remove the skewer. This is a striking way to serve them for a buffet or plated dinner.

DESSERTS AND SWEETS

Chocolate-Cherry Pound Cake à la mode with Drunken Tart Cherries

MAKES 8 SERVINGS

Chocolate and cherries are a classic combo. Dried Northwest cherries are available in both dark sweet and tart red varieties. I like to use the tart ones in this cake to contrast with the richness of the chocolate. The Chukar Cherry Company, located in the Columbia Valley of Eastern Washington, has been producing all-natural choice dried cherries since 1988.

Cake

8 tablespoons (1 stick) butter, softened

1 cup sugar

2 eggs

1 teaspoon vanilla extract

1½ cups flour

¼ cup unsweetened cocoa powder (regular, not Dutch process)

1½ teaspoons baking powder

½ teaspoon baking soda

¼ teaspoon salt

½ cup milk

¾ cup dried tart cherries

1 cup (6 ounces) bittersweet chocolate chips or chunks

Glaze

½ cup (3 ounces) bittersweet chocolate chips or chunks

¼ cup heavy cream

Chocolate cherry ice cream or other ice cream of your choice

Drunken Tart Cherries (facing page)

Preheat an oven to 350°F. Butter and flour a 5-by-9¼-inch nonstick loaf pan and set aside.

To make the cake, cream the butter and sugar in a large mixing bowl with an electric mixer until very fluffy. Beat in the eggs, one at a time, until thoroughly incorporated, scraping down the sides of the bowl often. Beat in the vanilla.

In a small bowl, mix the flour, cocoa, baking powder, baking soda, and salt.

With the mixer on low speed, add the flour mixture, in three parts, to the butter mixture alternately with the milk, beginning and ending with the flour mixture. Mix only until well combined; do not overmix.

Remove the bowl from the mixer and fold in the cherries and chocolate chips. Scrape the batter into the prepared pan, filling evenly. Rap the pan sharply on a counter several times to release any air bubbles, then smooth the surface of the batter.

Bake for about 50 to 60 minutes, or until a toothpick inserted in the center comes out clean. Rotate the pan after the first 30 minutes of baking.

Unmold the cake and turn it right-side up. Let cool thoroughly on a wire rack before glazing.

To make the glaze, in a small saucepan or in a microwave oven, gently heat the chocolate and cream until the chocolate is just melting. Remove from the heat and stir until the chocolate is thoroughly melted and mixture is smooth. Let cool to almost room temperature but still liquid. Pour over the cooled cake. Let the glaze set for 15 minutes before serving.

To serve, slice the cake into 16 slices and serve 2 slices, shingled, per serving. Top with a scoop of ice cream and a spoonful of cherries with their syrup.

Drunken Tart Cherries

MAKES 1 CUP

1 cup pitted dried tart cherries
¼ cup amaretto liqueur
3 tablespoons sugar
¼ cup boiling water

Mix the cherries, amaretto, and sugar in a small bowl. Pour the boiling water over the cherries and stir well. Cover and let sit at room temperature for at least 12 hours before using. Store, refrigerated, for up to 2 months.

CHEF'S NOTE: The Drunken Tart Cherries also make a delightful garnish for an ice-cold Manhattan!

Mini Blackberry Patch Tarts

MAKES 8 MINI TARTS

Oregon is the biggest blackberry producer in the United States, but the berries also grow wild all over the Northwest. Whether you comb the side streets in search of big, fat "railroad" berries (as my grandmother called them), cultivate marionberries in your backyard, or buy blackberries from the store, you'll find they're all delicious made into these mini tarts—just the thing to take to a summer barbecue or even a late Sunday brunch.

Crust

1$\frac{1}{2}$ cups flour

1 tablespoon minced lemon zest

1 teaspoon sugar

6 tablespoons cold butter, cut into
    small chunks

1 egg, beaten

2 teaspoons cider vinegar

2$\frac{1}{2}$ tablespoons ice water, plus more
    as needed

Filling

3 cups fresh blackberries

6 tablespoons sugar, or more to taste

2 teaspoons flour

1 teaspoon water

Sugar for sprinkling (optional)

To make the crust, mix the flour, lemon zest, and sugar in a large bowl. Scatter the butter on the surface of the flour, then, with a pastry blender or clean hands, combine until mixture forms pea-size particles.

In a small bowl, mix 1 tablespoon of the beaten egg (reserve the rest for egg wash), the vinegar, and the 2$\frac{1}{2}$ tablespoons ice water. Stir the liquid mixture into the flour mixture with a fork, mixing just until the liquid is incorporated. (The dough should be fairly moist and pliable, not crumbly. If the dough is too dry, then add more ice water, 1 to 2 teaspoons at a time.)

Form the dough into a log and wrap in plastic wrap. Chill in the refrigerator for 10 to 20 minutes if the kitchen temperature is very warm.

To make the filling, right before assembling the tarts, put the berries in a large bowl and sprinkle with the sugar and flour. Set aside.

To assemble and bake the tarts, preheat an oven to 400°F. Line a baking sheet with parchment paper or spray lightly with vegetable-oil cooking spray.

Cut the chilled dough into 8 equal portions. Working with 1 piece of dough at a time, press the portion into a flat disk. On a lightly floured surface, roll out the disk into a round, $\frac{1}{8}$ inch thick and 5 inches in diameter, pressing in the sides as needed to keep it round. Cover the rolled-out dough with plastic while you roll out the remaining pieces.

Toss the filling well. Divide the filling evenly among the rolled tart shells, heaping it in the center of each. Gather up the crust edges around the filling, bringing about 1 inch of the dough over the fruit and pinching it as needed to make an open-faced, rustic-looking tart. Be careful not to get any holes in the crust. If the crust tears, pinch it shut; you don't want the juices to run out! With a spatula, carefully transfer each tart to the baking sheet.

Whisk the water into the reserved beaten egg and lightly brush the exposed dough of the tarts with the egg wash. Sprinkle the tart tops lightly with sugar, if desired.

Bake for 35 to 40 minutes, or until the crust is golden brown and the filling is bubbling. (The cooking time will vary with different ovens.)

CHEF'S NOTE: If you make these in advance, let them cool, then put a piece of waxed paper or parchment paper loosely over them to hold for up to 2 days at room temperature. Do not refrigerate or cover them tightly. I like to reheat them slightly in a preheated 450°F oven for a couple of minutes and serve with a small scoop of vanilla ice cream.

BERRIES

Berries thrive in the Pacific Northwest, with our fertile soil, spring rains, and summers that bring hot days and cool evenings. There are dozens of indigenous berry species as well as the many kinds introduced by Europeans. Berries have long been a well-loved food that signals the beginning of summer.

Native Americans made pemmican, a cake of crushed berries, melted fat, and dried deer meat. And Northwest tribes also whipped up bittersweet soapberries with variegated-peach-colored salmonberries and water in a deep bowl until thick and frothy to make soapberry froth, or "Indian ice cream."

Generally the first to ripen are salmonberries and diminutive wild strawberries. Next, everyone yearns for the first lush locally grown strawberries; although their season is short, they are incredibly long on flavor and sweetness.

Later, the native trailing dewberries, known as wild mountain blackberries, mature. They range throughout the region north to south and from the Pacific coast to mountain slopes. Every summer, pickers scour the Cascades and Olympics to pluck these teeny tiny, unforgettable dainties. Another native bramble is the black raspberry, or blackcap; while its juice might be spare, the color is darker than night and the taste ambrosial.

Farmers' markets soon abound with cultivated "cane berries": raspberries in red, black, and golden yellow, and the many strains of blackberries and their cousins— marionberries, boysenberries, loganberries, and tayberries. And Mother Nature always provides a generous supply of "gone wild" blackberries, both evergreen and Himalayan. Many backyards have heirloom raspberries growing. Big, juicy, dark red, and intense, these berries might not look as flawless as some of the new "hybrids," but they exude flavor like you've never had before. A handful of these rouge babies will make you sit up straight and say "raspberry," or fall over swooning. There are only a few areas of the world where cane berries flourish, and the Northwest is assuredly the center of that universe.

Around the same time, plump blueberries start showing up on our tables, usually by the Fourth of July. There are more than a dozen species native to the region, and they are widely cultivated as well. In the same family is the huckleberry; its many species are found from the coast to the timberline.

Along the way come brilliant green gooseberries, wild and domesticated currants, thimbleberries, blue elderberries, the old-fashioned lingonberries brought by Scandinavian and German settlers, and the Canadian favorite, Saskatoons, or serviceberries.

All these berry options send pastry chefs into a frenzy to slump, grunt, cobble, and crisp their way through the summer as they whip up delicious baked treats. And we have still more berries, such as Oregon grape, salal, and elderberry, that—though a bit too tart for eating out of hand—make very pleasing jam, jelly, and wine.

Then in the fall comes the crimson cranberry. Early American sailing vessels carried this North American native berry, which is high in vitamin C, to prevent scurvy, and colonial recipes using them date back to the eighteenth century. The cranberry gets its name from Dutch and German settlers who called it the "crane berry" because of the way its pink flower petals twist back, resembling the head and bill of the sandhill crane. Over the years, the name was shortened to cranberry.

The Pacific Northwest is one of the major cranberry-growing areas. A compatible use of wetlands, cranberry farming provides habitat for many birds as well as other animals and plants.

Look for these tart, jewel-like berries in a fluffy oversized muffin alongside your morning latte. They are also a perfect foil for their seasonal cousins, pear and apple, in salads tossed with a blushing pink cranberry vinaigrette. And they're delicious in a piquant chutney cozied up to a roasted chicken or in a fragrant apple-cranberry tart. What more could you ask for from the season's last berry!

Buttermilk Panna Cotta with Cascade Berries

MAKES 6 SERVINGS

There's no better ending to a long summer day than a luscious berry dessert, especially if you have picked the berries yourself. The Northwest has a large variety of berries to choose from—including big, plump Himalayan blackberries that grow along city streets and country roads, currants, wild blackcap raspberries, and tiny wild pink and purple huckleberries.

Panna Cotta

1 envelope (1 scant tablespoon) unflavored gelatin

2 tablespoons warm water

1 cup heavy whipping cream

2 cups buttermilk

1/2 cup sugar

2 teaspoons poppy seed

Berries

2 cups mixed fresh berries, such as strawberries, raspberries, currants, blueberries, huckleberries, and blackberries

1/4 cup sugar, or to taste

1 tablespoon fresh lemon juice

To make the panna cotta, sprinkle the gelatin over the water in a large heatproof bowl. Let sit for 10 minutes.

Whisk in the cream, buttermilk, and sugar and set the bowl over a pan of simmering water. Whisk the mixture until smooth and the sugar is melted. Whisk in the poppy seed.

Divide the mixture evenly among 6 small glass custard dishes. Put the dishes on a baking sheet and cover with plastic wrap. Be sure the wrap does not touch the tops of the panna cotta. Refrigerate overnight, or for a minimum of 12 hours, before serving.

To prepare the berries, combine the fruit in a medium bowl and sprinkle with the sugar and lemon juice. (If using strawberries, quarter or slice them if large.) Stir, then let sit for 20 minutes before serving.

One at a time, place each ramekin of panna cotta in a shallow bowl of very hot water—to 1/2 inch from the top—for a count of about 10. Remove, run a knife around the outside, then unmold the panna cotta onto individual dessert plates. Spoon the berries and their juice on and around the panna cotta and serve immediately.

CHEF'S NOTE: You can make the panna cotta up to 3 days before serving, then prepare the berries 20 minutes ahead. I like to serve this dessert with tiny glasses of local berry liqueur.

Roasted Rhubarb Honey Mousse

This dessert was inspired by my mom—who every spring and early summer had a pan of sweetened rhubarb stewing. We used to have it for breakfast to top our oatmeal or spoon up on our toast. Rhubarb is also called "pie plant" after its most common usage, either on its own or with apples or strawberries, its best flavor partner. For this recipe, sugared rhubarb is slow-roasted to a syrupy goodness. While spooning the dreamy dessert slowly onto your tongue, you might wonder, "How did those tart-and-puckery stalks end up so heavenly?"

1 pound rhubarb, trimmed and cut into
   1-inch pieces (4 cups)
1 cup sugar
1 small package (3 ounces) cream cheese
5 tablespoons honey
1½ cups whipping cream

Garnishes
Whipped cream (optional)
Edible flowers (optional)

Preheat an oven to 375°F.

Toss the rhubarb and sugar together in a large bowl, then spread in a 9-by-13-inch glass baking dish. Roast, uncovered, for about 45 minutes, or until the rhubarb is soft and the syrup is slightly caramelized. Stir thoroughly and carefully after the first 20 minutes.

Let cool to room temperature, then refrigerate until chilled.

Whip the cream cheese with 4 tablespoons (¼ cup) of the honey in a mixer until very fluffy. Transfer to a large bowl and fold in the chilled rhubarb mixture. Whip the cream with the remaining tablespoon of honey until firmly peaked. Stir about one third of the whipped cream into the rhubarb mixture to lighten it, then fold in the remaining whipped cream.

Dish up into 6 pretty glasses. Refrigerate until ready to serve, then top, if desired, with a little plain whipped cream and an edible spring flower, such as a pansy, or petals of apple, pear, or plum blossoms.

CHEF'S NOTE: If selecting flowers from your yard, be sure that they are edible and have not been sprayed with pesticide or other chemicals. Rinse all blossoms thoroughly.

Bittersweet Chocolate Bread Pudding with Raspberry Drizzle

MAKES 8 TO 10 SERVINGS

In today's bread pudding, a good bread is the foundation ingredient, and with the many artisan bakeries in the Northwest, it isn't a chore to find a wonderful loaf. The challenge is in deciding which one to use! And if the bread's just a little bit stale, that's okay. In fact, bread pudding is a delicious way to use up day-old hand-crafted breads. For the chocolate sauce, try to find Fran's Dark Chocolate Sauce, from Seattle's nationally famed chocolatier, Fran Bigelow. It's just like a melted truffle!

2 cups heavy whipping cream

2 cups half-and-half

4 ounces bittersweet chocolate, chopped

10 egg yolks

3/4 cup granulated sugar

1/2 cup packed brown sugar

1 teaspoon vanilla extract

1 teaspoon ground cinnamon

1/4 teaspoon ground nutmeg

12 cups 1/2 - to 1-inch pieces hearty bread

1/3 cup chocolate sauce

3/4 cup pecan pieces (optional)

Raspberry Drizzle (recipe follows)

In a medium, heavy saucepan, warm the cream, half-and-half, and chocolate over medium heat, stirring until the chocolate is just barely melted. Meanwhile, in a large bowl, whisk the egg yolks, sugars, vanilla, and spices. Remove the chocolate mixture from the heat and whisk it slowly into the egg mixture. Fold the bread into the mixture and let it sit for 30 minutes until the bread is thoroughly soaked with the custard.

Meanwhile, preheat an oven to 325°F. Butter a 9-by-13-inch glass baking dish or a 3- to 3 1/2 -quart casserole dish, or spray with vegetable-oil cooking spray.

Spread the bread mixture evenly in the dish, drizzle with the chocolate sauce, then distribute the pecans (if using) over the top.

Bake for about 45 to 50 minutes, or until just set. Serve warm. Or, let cool and refrigerate until ready to serve, then reheat, covered, in a preheated 325°F oven for about 15 minutes until warmed.

Serve with Raspberry Drizzle.

Raspberry Drizzle

MAKES ABOUT 1 CUP

2 cups fresh or thawed frozen raspberries

1/2 cup sugar

2 tablespoons fresh lemon juice

Combine all the ingredients in a blender or food processor and process until the berries are puréed and the sugar is thoroughly dissolved. Strain through a fine-meshed sieve. You can make this up to 2 days in advance. If made ahead, refrigerate until ready to use.

CHEF'S NOTE: I also like to serve this with fresh raspberries if in season or with a dollop of whipped cream or a scoop of chocolate raspberry ice cream.

Fresh Mint Ice Cream with Chocolate Mint Candies

MAKES ABOUT 4 CUPS

Frango mint candies are a Northwest icon originally made in 1918 by the Fredrick & Nelson Company in Seattle. At the now-closed department store, you could not only buy these delicious candies but also enjoy them in the famous Frango milkshakes. Frangos are a creamy smooth chocolate mint confection with a hint of salt, which gives them that magical taste. You can purchase the candy, still available today, or try my recipe to make a version at home.

4 cups heavy whipping cream

3/4 cup sugar

1 1/2 cups packed mint sprigs, plus 2 tablespoons finely chopped fresh mint

6 egg yolks

1 cup coarsely chopped Chocolate Mint Candies (recipe follows) or Frango Mint candies

CHEF'S NOTE: I like to serve this garnished with a bit more chopped mint candy and a fresh sprig of mint.

Combine the cream and sugar in a large, heavy saucepan. Tear the mint sprigs (to bruise them) and add to the cream mixture. Bring to a slow simmer over medium heat.

In a bowl, whisk the egg yolks, then gradually whisk in about 1 cup of the hot cream mixture. Whisk the egg mixture into the cream. Whisking constantly, bring to a bare simmer and cook for about 30 seconds. Remove from the heat and whisk frequently to cool to room temperature. Refrigerate for at least 2 hours.

Strain the mixture and discard the mint leaves. Stir in the chopped mint, then pour into an ice cream maker and freeze according to manufacturer's instructions. Just before the ice cream is finished, stir in the chopped candies. Transfer the ice cream to a plastic container and freeze until ready to serve.

Chocolate Mint Candies

MAKES 24 NICE-SIZED PIECES, OR ENOUGH FOR 1 RECIPE OF ICE CREAM PLUS 12 EXTRA PIECES OF CANDY

12 ounces bittersweet chocolate, chopped

6 tablespoons butter

1/2 teaspoon salt

1/2 teaspoon peppermint extract

1/2 cup confectioners' sugar

In a medium bowl or double boiler, melt the chocolate, butter, salt, and peppermint extract together over a pan of barely simmering water, whisking until the chocolate is just melted. Remove from the heat, sift in the confectioners' sugar, then stir to combine well. Spread the mixture in an 8-inch square baking pan.

Let cool at room temperature for at least 4 hours, or refrigerate to harden faster.

To remove the candy from the pan, invert the pan onto a piece of plastic wrap or a cutting board, lay a hot towel over the pan bottom for about 1 minute, then tap the bottom of the pan. Loosen the candy with a spatula if needed. Cut the candy into 24 pieces to serve as candy, or coarsely chop to use in ice cream. Store refrigerated for up to 2 weeks.

STONE FRUITS

Oregon, Washington, and British Columbia all produce peaches, nectarines, apricots, plums, and cherries in brilliant hues. For locals, the stone fruit harvest might conjure up childhood memories of summer canning: sterilizing dozens of jars, then blanching, peeling, pitting, and packing the season's bounty. Rows and rows of colorful, artfully packed jars filled with pepper-pickled peaches—freestone Elbertas or juicy clings—rosy Tilton apricots, mustardy pickled-vegetable chowchow, and brandied Bing cherries lined the pantry and cellar shelves of Northwest homes.

These days, with busy work schedules, it's harder to find the home-canned jar of fruit tucked in a cupboard. But that doesn't mean all those thirst-quenching fruits aren't still enjoyed with abandon. And there's no reason to restrict the sweet orbs to the dessert course.

Cherries make for fantastically refreshing drinks and scintillating salsas. The one drawback to cooking with cherries is getting the seeds out, and this can be the pits!

If you are pitting a lot of cherries, get a large-volume pitter such as the one sold at Sur La Table (see page 223). It clamps easily onto the side of a picnic table—and outdoors is the ideal place to do this messy chore. Be sure to wear an old shirt; cherry stains are hard to get out, and by the time you are finished, you are usually freckled with pink dots!

Many Northwest chefs pair fruit and seafood with delicious results, one treatment being to pan-sear salmon with wedges of juicy peaches along with toasted hazelnuts and brown butter. Or you might see grilled salmon with apricot coulis or cherry salsa, Dungeness crab cakes with a sweet-and-sour plum beurre blanc, or coriander-dusted calamari with a nectarine-jalapeño dipping sauce.

Sunny peach orchard, Hood River, Oregon

Stone-Fruit Almond Shortcake with Brown Sugar Whipped Cream

Luscious, succulent stone fruits . . . any combination will make a brilliant shortcake topping. Just be sure they are super-ripe and juicy. Almonds are a natural pairing with stone fruits, so the not-too-sweet, nutty scone gives this American summer classic a fun and tasty twist.

6 cups mixed sliced ripe stone fruits, such as apricots, peaches, plums, cherries, and nectarines

1 cup sugar, or to taste

1 cup heavy whipping cream

¼ cup packed brown sugar

1 to 2 tablespoons amaretto liqueur (optional)

6 Almond Scones (recipe follows)

In a large bowl, sprinkle the fruit with sugar. Mix gently, then let sit for about 30 minutes to "juice up."

Meanwhile, in a chilled bowl, whip the cream and brown sugar together with a whisk or an electric mixer until the cream forms soft peaks. Be careful not to overwhip. Fold in the amaretto (if using). Refrigerate until ready to use.

To serve, split the scones and place the bottoms on plates. Divide the fruit mixture among the scones and top with the whipped cream. Place the scone tops back on, slightly askew.

Almond Scones

MAKES 8 SCONES

2¼ cups flour

¼ cup sugar

¾ teaspoon baking soda

½ teaspoon salt

½ teaspoon ground cinnamon

8 tablespoons (1 stick) butter

¼ cup sliced almonds

1 egg

¾ cup buttermilk, plus more if needed

1 egg white

½ teaspoon water

CHEF'S NOTE: Serve 6 scones for dessert and then you'll have 2 extra for breakfast or seconds!

Preheat an oven to 375°F. Sift the flour, sugar, baking soda, salt, and cinnamon together into a large bowl. Cut in the butter with a pastry blender or 2 dinner knives until the mixture is the texture of coarse crumbs (just like making a pie crust). Stir in the almonds.

In a separate bowl, whisk the whole egg with the ¾ cup buttermilk until blended. Make a well in the center of the flour mixture and pour the liquid into it. Combine with a few swift strokes. The dough should form a ball and all the flour should be incorporated. (If the dough is way too dry, add 1 tablespoon more buttermilk.) Do not overmix.

On a lightly floured surface, pat the dough into a ¾-inch-thick round. Place on an ungreased baking sheet, then cut into 8 wedges, leaving the sides touching.

In a small bowl, whisk the egg white and water until mixed, then brush the dough lightly with the egg white glaze.

Bake for 30 to 35 minutes, or until the scones are cooked through and golden. Let cool slightly before serving.

Mexican Spiced Hot Chocolate

MAKES 1 SERVING

Spicy cocoas are popping up more and more at local avant-garde espresso shops. In addition to the traditional hints of almond and cinnamon in this hot chocolate, I've included ancho chiles for their deep, rich flavor and slight kick. Not too hot, not too sweet—but just right—it will keep you coming back for sip after sip.

About 3 tablespoons Mexican Spiced Hot Chocolate Mix, depending on how chocolaty you like your cocoa (recipe follows)

¾ cup hot milk

Garnishes

Sweetened whipped cream

Ground cinnamon for sprinkling

Place the chocolate mix in a serving cup and then stir in the hot milk, mixing well. Top with a pouf of sweetened whipped cream and a sprinkle of cinnamon.

Mexican Spiced Hot Chocolate Mix

MAKES 2 CUPS, ENOUGH FOR 10 TO 12 SERVINGS

1¼ cups superfine sugar

1 teaspoon almond extract

¾ cup unsweetened Dutch process cocoa powder

2 teaspoons ground cinnamon

4 teaspoons ancho chile powder

1 teaspoon ground coriander

In a medium bowl, thoroughly whisk the sugar and almond extract. Add the remaining ingredients and whisk thoroughly.

Store at room temperature for up to 3 months in a clean glass jar with a tight lid. Shake thoroughly before using to remix the ingredients.

S'mores Cookies with Seattle Espresso Martini "on the side"

Cookies and . . . coffee? Well, kind of. Nicknamed Latte Land, Seattle loves its coffee, and these days the espresso shot is even showing up in dessert cocktails. Hey, you have to have something to dip that cookie in!

Dough

8 tablespoons (1 stick) butter, softened
¼ cup vegetable shortening
½ cup granulated sugar
½ cup packed brown sugar
1 egg
1 teaspoon vanilla extract
1½ cups flour
½ cup unsweetened cocoa powder
¾ teaspoon baking soda
½ teaspoon salt
One 8-ounce package toffee baking bits

Topping

1 cup mini marshmallows
¼ cup sweetened condensed milk
¼ cup graham cracker crumbs

To make the cookie dough, in a mixing bowl, cream the butter, shortening, sugars, egg, and vanilla well. Sift the flour, cocoa, baking soda, and salt together in a small bowl. Mix into the butter mixture. Stir in the toffee bits.

In a large piece of plastic wrap, roll the dough into a 3-inch-diameter log with flat ends. Wrap well and refrigerate for at least 1 hour, or up to 3 days.

When ready to bake, preheat an oven to 350°F. Line 4 or 5 baking sheets with baking parchment (see Chef's Note, below).

While the oven is heating, make the topping. Combine the ingredients in a medium bowl and mix with a rubber spatula or spoon until the marshmallows are thoroughly coated. The mixture will be very sticky.

Cut the chilled dough into 10 equal slices. Place 2 or 3 slices on each prepared baking sheet. (When baked, these cookies spread to about a 5-inch diameter, so bake only 2 or 3 per pan.) In the center of each cookie, place about 1 heaping tablespoon of topping, using it all.

Bake the cookies for 18 to 20 minutes, or until just done. Let cool on the baking parchment until totally cooled and easy to remove.

CHEF'S NOTE: If you're short of baking sheets, just lay out the dough slices on additional pieces of baking parchment. When a pan of cookies is done, remove the pan from the oven, slide the parchment with the baked cookies onto a rack, place the next parchment sheet of dough on the pan, and bake.

Seattle Espresso Martini

MAKES 1 DRINK

1 ounce Starbucks coffee liqueur
1 ounce Amarula cream liqueur
1 shot espresso (about 1 ounce)
3 coffee beans for garnishing

Fill a cocktail shaker with ice. Measure in the liqueurs. Add the espresso. Cap and shake vigorously until very cold. Strain the drink into a large cocktail glass. Float the coffee beans in the drink for garnish.

Lemon–Poppy Seed Bundt Cake with Bursting Blueberry Compote

MAKES 10 TO 12 SERVINGS

British Columbia is the second largest cultivator of blueberries in the world, with almost all of the crop being raised in the Lower Fraser Valley. Once called star-berries for the five-pointed calyx left on the fruit's blossom end, these blue pearls have long been loved. On their journey to Oregon Country, Lewis and Clark found Native Americans smoke-drying wild blueberries to use with meats and stews during the winter months. I love blueberries in this old-fashioned compote, where they underscore their provocative flavor companion, the lemon.

Cake

8 ounces (2 sticks) butter, softened

1 cup sugar

3 eggs, separated

1 cup sour cream

2 tablespoons minced or grated lemon zest

1³/₄ cups flour

1 teaspoon baking powder

1 teaspoon baking soda

3 tablespoons poppy seed

2 tablespoons limoncello liqueur or
   substitute Triple Sec

Glaze

1 tablespoon minced or grated lemon zest

¹/₄ cup fresh lemon juice

¹/₃ cup sugar

2 tablespoons butter

2 tablespoons limoncello liqueur or
   substitute Triple Sec

Continued›

Preheat an oven to 350°F. Thoroughly butter a 2¹/₂-quart Bundt pan or spray with vegetable-oil cooking spray, being careful to grease all the creases. Then flour the pan and set aside.

To make the cake, using a stand mixer with a paddle attachment, cream the butter and sugar until fluffy. Mix in the egg yolks, one at a time, mixing each until it is incorporated. Mix in the sour cream and lemon zest.

Sift the flour, baking powder, and baking soda together into a small bowl. Add the flour mixture to the butter mixture in two batches, mixing on medium speed until just incorporated. Mix in the poppy seed and limoncello.

In a separate, clean mixing bowl, beat the egg whites with a whisk attachment on high speed until soft-peaked but not dry.

Remove the bowl with the cake batter from the mixer and, using a large rubber spatula, add half of the whipped egg whites and carefully fold in. Add the remaining egg whites and fold in until incorporated. Scrape the batter into the prepared Bundt pan and tap the pan gently on a counter to release any air bubbles.

Bake for 35 to 40 minutes, or until a cake tester comes out clean. Remove from the oven and let cool in the pan on a wire rack for 10 minutes. Unmold, carefully running a knife around the edge to help release. Turn the cake over again so the pretty side shows and let cool thoroughly on the rack.

While the cake is cooling, make the glaze. In a small saucepan, bring the lemon zest and juice and sugar to a boil over high heat and boil for about 1 minute to reduce to ¹/₄ cup. Remove from the heat and whisk in the butter and limoncello. When the cake is completely cool, poke it in a few places with a toothpick, then drizzle half of the glaze over the cake. Let set for 5 minutes, then drizzle on the remaining glaze.

Continued›

Bursting Blueberry Compote

3 cups fresh blueberries

1/3 cup sugar

2 tablespoons water

1 tablespoon fresh lemon juice

To make the compote, combine the ingredients in a small saucepan and cook over medium heat until the blueberry skins have popped and the mixture is slightly thickened, about 6 to 8 minutes. Let cool, or refrigerate until ready to serve. (Bring to room temperature before serving.)

To serve, cut the cake into thick slices and dollop each serving with some of the compote.

CHEF'S NOTE: This cake is glorious also dolloped with a pouf of lightly sweetened whipped cream or scoops of lavender ice cream. And the cake is outstanding to serve for breakfast or brunch with coffee.

Jewel Fruit-Studded Oatmeal Cookies

MAKES ABOUT 32 COOKIES

Crisp but still chewy, these cookies are studded with an assortment of gem-colored dried fruits of the Northwest. If you want them extra-fruity, you can add more varieties, such as dried blueberries and chopped dried pears and peaches.

8 ounces (2 sticks) butter, softened

1 cup packed brown sugar

1 cup granulated sugar

2 eggs

1 1/2 cups flour

1/4 teaspoon salt

1/4 teaspoon ground cinnamon

1/4 teaspoon ground nutmeg

1 teaspoon baking soda

1 teaspoon vanilla extract

3 cups rolled oats (old-fashioned or quick-cooking, but not instant)

1/2 cup chopped dried sweet or tart cherries

2/3 cup chopped dried apricots

1/2 cup dried cranberries

1/4 cup dried currants

In a large bowl, cream the butter and sugars together until light. Add the eggs and mix until well combined. Scrape down the sides of the bowl, then add the flour, salt, spices, baking soda, vanilla, and oats and mix on low speed until thoroughly combined. Stir in the dried fruit to distribute evenly. Chill the dough in the refrigerator for 20 minutes.

Meanwhile, preheat an oven to 375°F and grease baking sheets or spray with vegetable-oil cooking spray. Drop tablespoons of dough 3 inches apart on the prepared baking sheets and flatten each spoonful with your fingertips.

Bake for 12 to 14 minutes, or until the edges of the cookies are browned. Rotate the pans halfway through baking. Let the cookies cool on the pans for 5 minutes before transferring to a wire rack to cool completely.

COFFEE

Seattle—and right along with it the rest of the Northwest—is coffee-crazy.

In 1971, Starbucks Coffee opened its first store in the Pike Place Public Market, bringing Seattle dark-roasted whole beans and influencing the future of our coffee culture. It was those dark-roasted beans that started the love affair with the rich smooth cups of "joe" that Northwesterners are so passionate about. The Northwest's nationally acclaimed coffee roasters roast their beans very dark, changing the sugar and starches in green coffee beans and releasing the volatile oils that give coffee a lot of its rich flavor and, to a coffee devotee, intoxicating aroma.

Where other cities have a hot-dog cart on every corner, Seattle has an espresso cart. You can even get your favorite espresso drink without ever leaving your car, as there is a drive-through kiosk positioned at just about every heavily trafficked location.

Not only are there carts galore, but there has developed an almost cult-like coffee lingo. Pass by a busy espresso stand in downtown Seattle, Portland, or Vancouver early some morning and you might hear something like this: "I'll have a double half-caf, short cappuccino, skinny." To those not in the know, that means a double shot of espresso (one regular, the other decaffeinated) with a short topping of low-fat steamed-milk foam.

Perhaps the long, gray days have brought about a kind of espresso madness in the region. Not only does the Northwest like its caffeine for a quick rainy-day pick-me-up, but chefs and mixologists incorporate it into our desserts and cocktails, such as my S'mores Cookies with Seattle Espresso Martini "on the side" (page 211): a super-caffeinated, adult version of cookies and milk. And coffee is put in some other pretty peculiar places, too, from espresso shots in barbecue sauce (which is actually amazingly good) to fine grounds in a salt rub for grilled steaks. Eugene City Brewing even makes a Coffee Stout!

Washington Apple-Cranberry Tart with Walnut Crust & Cranberry Semifreddo

MAKES 10 SERVINGS

Apple pie is of course a regional emblem, but this recipe takes it to a bit more sophisticated level—with a tempting tart presentation and walnut crust. I like to use the Gala, a firm, sweet-tart apple, for its ability to keep its shape when baked. Fluffy, creamy semifreddo made with local cranberries provides a nice tart-sweet counterbalance.

Filling

1 tablespoon butter

4 pounds Gala apples, peeled, cored, and cut into ¼-inch-thick wedges (6 cups)

½ cup fresh or frozen cranberries

2 tablespoons brandy

2 teaspoons fresh lemon juice

½ cup sugar

2 teaspoons ground cinnamon

Crust

8 ounces (2 sticks) unsalted butter at room temperature

¾ cup granulated sugar

¼ cup packed brown sugar

2 teaspoons vanilla extract

3 egg yolks

1 egg, separated

2½ cups flour

¼ teaspoon salt

½ cup very finely chopped walnuts

2 tablespoons sanding or coarse sugar

Cranberry Semifreddo (page 218)

10 fresh or frozen cranberries for garnishing

To make the filling, heat the butter in a large saucepan over medium-high heat and add the apples and cranberries. Stir in the brandy and lemon juice, then the sugar and cinnamon. Cook until the apples are just wilted but still firm, and the juices have evaporated and cooked out; the mixture should be almost dry. Transfer to a shallow pan and cool in the refrigerator while making the crust.

Preheat an oven to 350°F. Line the bottom of a 9- or 10-inch springform pan with a parchment round. Lightly butter the sides of the pan and the parchment, or spray with vegetable-oil cooking spray. Set aside.

To make the crust, in a mixing bowl, beat the butter with the sugars on medium-high speed with an electric mixer until light and fluffy, about 3 minutes. Scrape down the sides of the bowl, then add the vanilla and the 4 egg yolks, one at a time, beating a few seconds after each. Beat until smooth and light, about 1 minute. (Reserve the egg white.)

In a medium bowl, mix the flour, salt, and walnuts, then add the flour mixture to the egg mixture in 2 parts, mixing on low until just combined.

Divide the dough into 2 equal pieces. Put one piece into the prepared pan and press it out evenly on the bottom and up 1½ inches on the sides. (If the dough is too soft to work with, wrap in plastic wrap and refrigerate for 10 to 20 minutes.) Pile the cooled filling into the dough-lined pan.

On a lightly floured surface such as a big piece of plastic wrap, press the remaining piece of dough into a round 9 or 10 inches in diameter, depending on the size of your pan. Slide the dough onto the filling and press it into place. This top crust should fit just inside the dough that extends up the sides of the pan and come all the way to its edges. Carefully seal the seam where the top joins the side dough, making sure the edges are straight and even.

Whip the egg white in a bowl until frothy. Brush the top crust with the egg white and poke the top with a fork in 5 places. Sprinkle with the sanding sugar.

Continued›

Bake for 50 to 60 minutes, or until the crust is golden brown and the filling is bubbling out a bit. Cool to room temperature before removing the pan sides. You might want to run a knife along the sides before unmolding. (When serving, be sure that the parchment paper is not stuck to the tart.)

To serve, slice the tart into 10 wedges. Place each wedge on a dessert plate. Top with a nice scoop of the semifreddo and garnish with a cranberry.

Cranberry Semifreddo

MAKES ABOUT 10 SERVINGS

Cranberries grow in sandy, acidic peat soils known as bogs. In the Northwest, many of the more than 200 growers cultivate cranberry bogs started 150 years ago by Finnish farmers. A stretch of Washington Highway 105 around Grayland is even called the "Cranberry Coast." Every September and October, communities along the Pacific coast—from Bandon, Oregon, to the historic village of Fort Langley, British Columbia—hold cranberry festivals.

2 eggs, separated
½ cup fresh or frozen cranberries
2 tablespoons cranberry juice cocktail
½ cup granulated sugar
3 tablespoons mascarpone cheese
2 tablespoons superfine sugar
½ cup heavy whipping cream

Let the eggs come to room temperature while you proceed with the recipe.

Combine the cranberries, juice, and ¼ cup of the granulated sugar in a small saucepan over medium-high heat. Cook until the cranberries pop, about 3 minutes. Remove from the heat, let cool, then purée until smooth.

In a medium stainless-steel bowl, whisk the egg yolks, remaining ¼ cup granulated sugar, and cranberry purée. Set the bowl over a pan of simmering water, taking care that the bowl does not touch the water. Whisk until the mixture is thickened and hot—but be careful not to overcook (scramble) the egg mixture; this takes about 3 to 5 minutes. Remove from the heat and whisk in the mascarpone. Keep whisking until the mixture cools down, then refrigerate until thoroughly chilled.

Meanwhile, in a thoroughly clean and grease-free medium mixer bowl, whip the egg whites on high speed with an electric mixer until they just start to get frothy. Start sprinkling in the superfine sugar and whip until the whites are peaking. Gently fold the whipped egg whites into the chilled cranberry mixture.

Whip the cream until stiff, then gently fold it into the cranberry mixture, taking care not to lose volume.

Spoon the mixture into a 4-cup plastic container with a lid. Tap the container on a counter to release any bubbles, then smooth the top. Close the container, then place in a freezer for at least 8 hours, or until frozen.

Pink & Puffy Strawberry Chiffon Pie

MAKES ONE 9-INCH PIE, OR ABOUT 6 SERVINGS

Light, fluffy, and sooooo summery, chiffon pies are almost forgotten these days. I remember first making this in high-school home ec class and absolutely loving it. Today's "grown-up" version is most luxurious served with a small glass of berrylicious liqueur from Brandy Peak Distillery in Brookings, Oregon. This summer is the best time to finally make that perfect pie!

Crust

1½ cups very finely crushed vanilla wafer
   cookies

6 tablespoons butter, melted

¼ cup sugar

Filling

1 pint fresh strawberries, stemmed and sliced

¾ cup sugar

½ cup cranberry or cranberry-raspberry
   juice cocktail

1 envelope unflavored gelatin

½ cup heavy whipping cream

2 egg whites

Garnishes

Sweetened whipped cream

Fresh strawberries with stems, halved
   lengthwise

CHEF'S NOTE: The crumbs for the crust should be fine, like cornmeal. You can crush them in a food processor or seal them in a plastic bag and roll with a rolling pin.

To make the crust, preheat an oven to 375°F. Thoroughly mix the cookie crumbs, butter, and sugar in a medium bowl. Put the mixture in a 9-inch pie pan and press evenly into the pan bottom, then up the sides and out onto the rim. Bake for about 6 to 8 minutes, then let cool to room temperature.

To make the filling, combine the berries and ½ cup of the sugar in a food processor and just lightly pulse a couple of times to break up the berries—do not purée or chop fine. (If you don't have a food processor, use a potato masher or clean hands to do this.) Let the mixture sit for 10 minutes (no longer!) before continuing.

Meanwhile, in a small saucepan, stir the cranberry juice and gelatin together. Stir the mixture over low heat until the gelatin is just dissolved, then pour into a large bowl and set aside to let cool.

Add the strawberry mixture to the cooled gelatin mixture. Refrigerate, stirring occasionally, until the mixture is partially set—gloppy but not firm. (This takes about 20 to 30 minutes, depending on your refrigerator.)

When the mixture is partially set, quickly whip the cream in a mixer until quite stiff and then refrigerate the cream while you whip the egg whites.

In a clean, grease-free mixer bowl, beat the egg whites on high speed until soft peaks form. Then very, very slowly add the remaining ¼ cup sugar, 1 tablespoon at a time, and beat until stiff, glossy peaks form.

Gently fold the egg whites into the strawberry mixture, then gradually and very gently fold in the cream. Working quickly, mound the filling in the cooled pie shell. Refrigerate the pie until the filling is firm, at least 3 hours.

Garnish with sweetened whipped cream and halved strawberries. Keep any leftover pie refrigerated for up to 2 days.

GLOSSARY

al dente: An Italian term referring to the stage of cooking reached when there is still a slight resistance to the teeth when the food is bitten. Pasta cooked al dente is just barely tender; no taste of raw flour remains.

arugula: A nutty, peppery green, also known as rocket or Italian cress. Arugula is commercially grown as well as naturalized in many areas. The blossoms are also edible. Substitute other peppery greens, such as watercress.

Asian pear: A sweet, mild-flavored pear resembling an apple in shape; it has a pale yellow, light tan, or reddish skin, and the flesh is white and very crisp and juicy. There are many varieties of Asian pear, also known as pear apple or Japanese pear.

black beans, salted: Small black soybeans that have been preserved in salt and have a strong salty flavor. Also known as fermented black beans or Chinese black beans, they are usually soaked and/or rinsed before using.

black mustard seed: Most commonly used in Middle Eastern cooking. Substitute yellow mustard seed.

black sesame seed: Jet black in color and used as a dramatic garnish. These are earthier tasting than white sesame seed and are available in Asian markets. Substitute white sesame seed.

capers: Pickled buds of the caper bush; used in sauces, dressings, and other dishes where a piquant flavor is wanted. Available packed in brine or salt; rinse capers that are packed in salt.

chèvre: Goat's-milk cheese. Most commonly available as a soft, spreadable cheese with a tangy flavor.

chipotle: A smoked, ripe jalapeño chile that is available dried, in chili powder form, or canned in adobo sauce.

cilantro: Also called Chinese parsley, Mexican parsley, or fresh coriander leaves. The leaves have a bold taste with sharp citrus notes.

clam, geoduck: This odd-looking king clam reaches sizes up to 3 feet including its protruding siphon, with average weights of 1 to 3 pounds. After cleaning, its siphon is enjoyed thinly sliced and served raw as sashimi; the body meat is thinly sliced and sautéed; the chopped meat is used in clam chowder.

clam, littleneck: A hard-shelled clam, native to the Pacific coast. Littlenecks and Manila clams are the typical steamer clams in the Northwest. Substitute any small, hard-shelled clam. Clams are fresh if shells are tightly closed or close quickly after tapping. Discard any that fail to open after cooking.

clam, razor: *Siliqua patula,* a long and narrow, square-edged-shell clam, ranging from 2 to 10 inches in length, with tender ivory meat. On the West Coast, it is typically dredged in flour and quickly fried.

clarified butter: Clarified butter is best for sautéing because the milk solids have been removed; therefore, it can be heated to a fairly high temperature without burning. To clarify butter, melt it in a small saucepan over low heat without stirring, then skim and discard any white foam. Spoon the clear butter into a container and reserve. Discard the milky residue.

coconut milk: Canned unsweetened coconut milk is available in Asian markets.

fish sauce: A staple seasoning as well as a condiment throughout Southeast Asia. Known as *nuoc nam* in Vietnam and *nam pla* in Thailand, this flavorful liquid is made by layering fresh anchovies with salt in wooden barrels and fermenting for several months.

green tomato: A tomato that is picked before it totally matures and turns red. Larger green tomatoes that are used for frying are typically picked when the skin just starts to get a bit of a pink tint.

hazelnut oil: Made from pressing hazelnuts, this oil is light brown and has a nutty flavor. Delicious in salad dressings.

juniper berries: The aromatic berries of the juniper tree or shrub. Often used in pickling-spice mixtures and in game cookery. Juniper berries provide the characteristic flavor of gin.

Kaffir lime leaf: This very fragrant leaf is typically available fresh and sometimes frozen from well-stocked Asian grocers. The leaves freeze well stored in a resealable plastic bag.

kalamata olives: Salty, brined Greek olives available in specialty foods markets and well-stocked delis.

lemongrass: Has a delicate, perfumey lemon aroma. Fresh lemongrass is sold by the stalk, which averages 1½ to 2 feet in length. If the lemongrass is to be eaten, only the lower part of the stalk is used for cooking, as the outer and top leaves are tough. The entire stalk can be used for flavoring or garnishing.

mushrooms, shiitake: Widely available fresh and dried in Asian markets and sometimes called Chinese black mushrooms. Substitute dried shiitakes only if fresh are not available; reconstitute by soaking in hot water.

mushrooms, wild: Any mixture of wild edible mushrooms, such as chanterelle, morel, boletus, hedgehog, or other delicious species too numerous to list. *Warning:* Always be sure purchased wild mushrooms come from a reliable source, or go with a mycology expert to identify mushrooms when picking your own. Be sure to thoroughly cook wild mushrooms; never eat them raw.

mustard, dry English: A mustard powder milled from white and brown mustard seeds; it is quite spicy.

panko: Japanese bread crumbs. When used to coat food for frying, they produce a light, crispy breading. Substitute cracker meal or fine dry bread crumbs.

reconstitute: To rehydrate a dried food by soaking in water or other cooking liquid.

rice, basmati: A delicious, nutty-flavored long-grain rice that is prepared by a variety of methods, from simple steaming to pilaf style. Most basmati rice is cultivated in India and Pakistan.

rice, Calrose: A medium-grain white rice variety. Once cooked, the kernels stick together. Used for Japanese-style plain steamed rice; it also absorbs other flavors well. Short-grain white rice can be substituted.

rice, jasmine: A very aromatic and flavorful rice that is especially popular in Thai cooking. It is also known as Thai fragrant rice and is typically simply steamed.

sake: A widely available Japanese rice wine. Substitute dry sherry.

sambal oelek: A Southeast Asian hot chili condiment. Substitute one quarter the amount of red pepper flakes or chili oil.

sauté: To cook quickly in a hot pan with a small amount of butter or oil.

sesame oil: Made from pressing sesame seed. Asian-style sesame oil is pressed from toasted sesame seed and is used primarily for its nutty flavor.

star anise: A beautiful eight-pointed star-shaped pod of a small evergreen that grows in southwestern China and northern Vietnam. It is available in Asian markets.

stocks and broths: Homemade stocks are definitely preferable, but high-quality canned and packaged beef and chicken stocks are a convenience, as is bottled clam juice, which is a handy substitute for fish stock. These products are usually salty, so season the recipe with care. If using homemade stocks, be sure they are very rich and well seasoned.

vinegar, rice: A white or pale-colored, mild-flavored Japanese vinegar; it comes in seasoned and unseasoned varieties.

vinegar, white balsamic: A light-colored version of balsamic vinegar. White balsamic is milder than traditional balsamic vinegar.

Walla Walla Sweet onion: A very sweet onion grown in a federally protected designated agricultural area that overlaps the Washington-Oregon border. Available June through September. Substitute any other sweet onion.

SOURCES

KathyCasey.Com

Visit my website store for my favorite cooking gadgets and foodie finds, as well as listings for TV and personal appearances, a seasonal newsletter, and recipes.

Kathy Casey Food Studios

5130 Ballard Avenue NW, Seattle, WA 98107
(206) 784-7840
www.kathycasey.com
Throw a Party, Toss a Salad, Take a Class or Celebrate in Style, all in One Spectacular Setting: Kathy Casey's unique venue and home for her consulting business, special events, team building, cooking and cocktail classes.

Dish D'Lish

Company Flagship Store opening 2006
5136 Ballard Avenue NW, Seattle, WA 98107
(206) 789-8121
www.kathycasey.com
A specialty food shop and café featuring Food T' Go Go: Dish D'Lish retail products, such as Cranberry Vinaigrette Dressing and Sour Cherry Ginger Chutney, gourmet meals to take home, and unique food finds.

Dish D'Lish

Seattle-Tacoma International Airport
(206) 433-5121
www.kathycasey.com
Sit-down cafés also featuring Food T' Go Go for hungry travelers. Two locations, one post-security in the Central Terminal, the other pre-security.

CHEESE

Pacific Northwest Cheese Project

www.pnwcheese.typepad.com
A fantastic website on Northwest cheeses, cheese makers, and cheese-related notions.

Quillisascut Cheese Company

2409 Pleasant Valley Road, Rice, WA 99167
(509) 738-2011
www.quillisascutcheese.com
A small family farm located at the base of the Huckleberry Mountain range, just off the Columbia River.

Sally Jackson Cheeses

16 Nealy Road, Oroville, WA 98844
(509) 485-3722
www.sallyjacksoncheeses.com
Farmstead cheeses are made from three kinds of milk: goat, cow, and sheep.

Estrella Family Creamery

659 Wynoochee Valley Road
Montesano, WA 98563
(360) 249-6541
A family-owned and -operated grass-based dairy, making hand-crafted old-world-style cheeses with cow's, goat's, and sheep's milk.

Samish Bay Cheese

P.O. Box 202, Bow, WA 98232
(360) 766-6707
cheese@rootabaga.com
Organic farmstead cheeses.

WSU Creamery

Washington State University
P.O. Box 641122, Pullman, WA 99164
(800) 457-5442
www.wsu.edu/creamery
Order their unique "canned" cheeses. My favorite is Cougar Gold.

Tillamook Cheese

4175 Highway 101 North
P.O. Box 313, Tillamook, OR 97141
(503) 815-1300
www.tillamookcheese.com
A farmer-owned cooperative whose claim to fame is its great Cheddar.

The Rogue Creamery

311 North Front Street
Central Point, OR 97502
(866) 665-1155
www.roguegoldcheese.com
Award-winning blue and Cheddar cheeses.

Artisanal Cheese Center

500 West 37th Street, New York, NY 10018
(877) 797-1200
www.artisanalcheese.com
International artisanal cheeses available by mail order. Excellent educational resource for cheese-lovers.

SPECIALTY PRODUCTS

Holmquist Hazelnut Orchards

9821 Holmquist Road, Lynden, WA 98264
(800) 720-0895
www.holmquisthazelnuts.com
Grown in the Nooksack River Valley, Holmquist hazelnuts are a sweeter, thinner-skinned variety of the hazelnut and are longer in shape.

Evergreen Orchards
3850 Three Mile Lane, McMinnville, OR 97128
(866) 434-4818
www.evergreenorchards.com
Oregon hazelnuts grown in the beautiful
Willamette Valley.

Fran's Chocolates
1300 East Pike, Seattle, WA 98122
mail-order: (800) 422-FRAN
www.franschocolates.com
Exceptional chocolates, caramels, and
chocolate sauces.

The Spanish Table
1427 Western Avenue, Seattle, WA 98101
(206) 682-2827
www.spanishtable.com
An excellent source for smoked paprika, this
shop also carries a wide variety of food and
cookware from Spain and Portugal.

Uwajimaya Market, Seattle
600 Fifth Avenue South, Seattle, WA 98104
(206) 624-6248
www.uwajimaya.com
A cornerstone of Seattle's International
District, Uwajimaya Village has become a
popular tourist and shopping destination for
Asian groceries, seafood, meats, and produce,
along with unique gifts.

Uwajimaya Market, Beaverton
10500 SW Beaverton-Hillsdale Highway
Beaverton, OR 97005
(503) 643-4512
www.uwajimaya.com
Uwajimaya Beaverton brings its selection of
Asian products and commitment to freshness
to the Greater Portland area.

Sur La Table
84 Pine Street, Seattle, WA 98101
(800) 243-0852
www.surlatable.com
Unique kitchenware, gadgets, and cookbooks.

Clear Creek Distillery
1430 NW 23rd Avenue, Portland, OR 97210
(503) 248-9470
www.clearcreekdistillery.com
Eau-de-vies made at their Northwest Portland
distillery exclusively from Oregon fruit.

World Spice Merchants
1509 Western Avenue, Seattle, WA 98101
(206) 682-7274
www.worldspice.com
Exceptional and unusual spices.

More Than Gourmet
929 Home Avenue, Akron, OH 44310
(800) 860-9385
www.morethangourmet.com
High-quality demi-glace and stock reductions.

Chukar Cherry Company
P.O. Box 510, Prosser, WA 99350
(800) 624-9544
www.chukar.com
Dried local cherries.

WINE

Pacific Coast Oyster Wine Competition
results can be found at
www.taylorshellfishfarms.com/oysterwine.

McCarthy & Schiering
2401B Queen Anne Avenue North
Seattle, WA 98109
(206) 282-8500
www.mccarthyandschiering.com
Specializing in wines from Washington and
Oregon.

Pike and Western Wine Shop
1934 Pike Place, Seattle, WA 98101
(206) 441-1307
www.pikeandwestern.com
Stocking a well-rounded selection of wines
from the Pacific Northwest.

Washington Wine Commission
Washington Wine Center
93 Pike Street, Suite 315, Seattle, WA 98101
(206) 667-9463
www.washingtonwine.org

British Columbia Wine Institute
1737 Pandosy Street, Kelowna, BC
Canada V1Y 1R2
(800) 661-2294
www.winebc.com

Oregon Wine Board
1200 NW Naito Parkway, Suite 400
Portland, OR 97209
(503) 228-8336
www.oregonwine.org

FISH & SHELLFISH

Mutual Fish
2335 Rainier Avenue South, Seattle, WA 98144
(206) 322-4368
www.mutualfish.com
Mutual Fish specializes in the freshest and
liveliest seafood available. In addition to
fresh and live products, they have their own
custom seafood products.

Taylor Shellfish Farms
2182 Chuckanut Drive, Bow, WA 98232
(360) 766-6002
www.taylorshellfish.com
The Taylor family has been growing shellfish
for over 100 years. They offer geoduck,
oysters, mussels, and clams.

Portlock
2821 NW Market Street, Seattle, WA 98107
(206) 781-7260
www.portchatham.com
Premium-quality smoked seafood.

Gerard & Dominique Seafoods
19726 144th Avenue NE, Woodinville, WA 98072
(800) 858-0449
www.gdseafoods.com
Epicurean smoked salmon.

Homer Alaska Halibut Derby
Homer Chamber of Commerce
P.O. Box 541, Homer, AK 99603
(907) 235-7740
www.homerhalibutderby.com
The Homer Jackpot Halibut Derby is the longest-running derby in Alaska and boasts the largest jackpot, too.

Alaska Seafood Marketing Institute
311 North Franklin Street, Suite 200
Juneau, AK 99801
(800) 478-2903
www.alaskaseafood.org

The Marine Stewardship Council
www.msc.org
The Marine Stewardship Council (MSC) is an independent nonprofit organization that promotes responsible fishing practices.

MUSHROOMS

Puget Sound Mycological Society
U.W. Center for Urban Horticulture
P.O. Box 354115, Seattle, WA 98195
(206) 522-6031
www.psms.org
An organization of people interested in mushrooms and mushrooming. It provides support and encouragement for research, education, cultivation, hunting, identifying, and cooking mushrooms.

Oregon Mycological Society
www.wildmushrooms.org
The purpose of the society is to study, collect, and identify fungi; to educate members and the public in fungi identification; and to promote health and safety in the gathering and consumption of fungi.

The Vancouver Mycological Society
101–1001 West Broadway
P.O. Box 181, Vancouver, BC, Canada V6H 4E4
(604) 878-9878
www.vanmyco.com
The VMS is a group of individuals who share a common interest in mushrooms and fungi. Monthly meetings.

Oregon White Truffles
www.oregonwhitetruffles.com
The history of Oregon white truffles.

Alaska Mycological Society
P.O. Box 2526, Homer, AK 99603

FARMERS' MARKETS & AGRICULTURE

BC Association of Farmers Markets
455B Alexander Avenue
Kamloops, BC
Canada V2B 3R5
www.bcfarmersmarket.org

Oregon's Farmers Markets Association
P.O. Box 215
Portland, OR 97207
(503) 233-8425
www.oregonfarmersmarkets.org

Washington State Farmers Market Association
P.O. Box 30727, Seattle, WA 98113
(206) 706-5198
www.wafarmersmarkets.com

Pike Place Market
85 Pike Street, Room 500, Seattle, WA 98101
(206) 682-7453
www.pikeplacemarket.org
Pike Place Market is internationally recognized as America's premier farmers' market. "The Market," as the locals affectionately call it, attracts ten million visitors a year, making it one of Washington's most frequently visited destinations.

Alaska Grown
www.alaskagrown.org
A list of Alaska's farmers' markets.

Alaska State Fair
2075 Glenn Highway, Palmer, AK 99645
(907) 745-4827
www.alaskastatefair.org
The Alaska State Fair site has a Large Vegetable List of record-setting giant vegetables!

MISCELLANEOUS

eGullet
Pacific Northwest and Alaska Forum
www.forums.egullet.org
A fantastic forum on Northwest cuisine, restaurants, and more.

Chowhound's Pacific Northwest Region
www.chowhound.com/pacificnw
Tasty discussions on Washington and Oregon restaurants and food finds.

Northwest Hot Springs
www.nwhotsprings.net
A web page for those who enjoy soaking in natural hot springs. The site includes information on sites, directions, and photos.

INDEX

TABLE OF EQUIVALENTS

The exact equivalents in the following tables have been rounded for convenience.

LIQUID/DRY MEASURES

U.S.	METRIC
¼ teaspoon	1.25 milliliters
½ teaspoon	2.5 milliliters
1 teaspoon	5 milliliters
1 tablespoon (3 teaspoons)	15 milliliters
1 fluid ounce (2 tablespoons)	30 milliliters
¼ cup	60 milliliters
⅓ cup	80 milliliters
½ cup	120 milliliters
1 cup	240 milliliters
1 pint (2 cups)	480 milliliters
1 quart (4 cups, 32 ounces)	960 milliliters
1 gallon (4 quarts)	3.84 liters
1 ounce (by weight)	28 grams
1 pound	454 grams
2.2 pounds	1 kilogram

LENGTH

U.S.	METRIC
⅛ inch	3 millimeters
¼ inch	6 millimeters
½ inch	12 millimeters
1 inch	2.5 centimeters

OVEN TEMPERATURE

FAHRENHEIT	CELSIUS	GAS
250	120	½
275	140	1
300	150	2
325	160	3
350	180	4
375	190	5
400	200	6
425	220	7
450	230	8
475	240	9
500	260	10